# Why You Nee[

**F**ew taxpayers are treated more harshly by IRS than gamblers. That's what Bill Remos found out. Remos, a Coca-Cola delivery driver in Chicago who also gambled for fun, got lucky: He won $50,000 in a single game of blackjack.

When Remos filed his taxes for the year he didn't report the $50,000 win as income. Why? He knew he had at least $50,000 in gambling losses during the year. He subtracted his losses from his winnings and ended up with zero; so he figured he didn't have any gambling income to list on his return. Makes sense, doesn't it? Not to the IRS.

Remos was audited by the IRS. Because he failed to follow the rules and couldn't document his losses, he had to pay income tax on his entire $50,000 blackjack win. He ended up owing the IRS $17,000 in back taxes. This on an annual income of only $32,000!

Bill Remos found out about the gambling tax rules the hard way. This book gives you all the information you need to avoid his unhappy fate. It can be used for any type of gambling, including:

- casino games such as slots, keno, blackjack, craps, and roulette
- internet gambling
- race track and dog track betting
- lotteries
- poker tournaments

- bingo
- raffles, and
- sports betting.

The tax rules covered in this book even apply to illegal gambling—yes, it's subject to taxation, too.

*You need to understand and follow these rules even if you lose more than you win during the year.* If you don't, you could end up like Bill Remos.

# Also by Stephen Fishman

*The Copyright Handbook: How to Protect and Use Written Works* (Nolo 1992)

*Software Development: A Legal Guide* (Nolo 1994)

*Copyright Your Software* (Nolo 1994)

*Working with Independent Contractors* (Nolo 1997)

*Working for Yourself: Law & Taxes for Consultants, Independent Contractors and Freelancers* (Nolo 1997)

*Consultant and Independent Contractor Agreements* (Nolo 1998)

*The Public Domain: How to Find and Use Copyright Free Writings, Music, Art and More* (Nolo 2001)

*Nondisclosure Agreements: Protect Your Trade Secrets & More* (Nolo 2001)

*The Inventor's Guide to Law and Business* (Nolo 2003)

*Deduct It: Save On Your Small Business Taxes* (Nolo 2004)

*Home Business Tax Deductions* (Nolo 2004)

*Every Landlord's Tax Deduction Guide* (Nolo 2004)

*Easy Ways to Lower Your Taxes* (Nolo 2006)

*Tax Deductions for Professionals* (Nolo 2007)

*Copyright and the Public Domain* (Law Journal Press 2008)

*Every Nonprofit's Tax Guide* (Nolo 2009)

*Nonprofit Fundraising Registration: The 50 State Guide* (Nolo Press 2010)

# All In Against the IRS: Every Gambler's Tax Guide

## STEPHEN FISHMAN, J.D.

Pipsqueak Press

www.pipsqueak-press.com

Pipsqueak

# All In Against the IRS: Every Gambler's Tax Guide

Published by:
Pipsqueak Press
Berkeley, California
www.pipsqueak-press.com

Copyright © 2011 by Stephen Fishman
ISBN 978-0-9832907-0-4
First Printing
February 2011

*Contact the Author:*

Comments and questions can be sent to the author at: stephenfishman@gmail.com

# Table of Contents

# The Rules of the Game

You have to know the rules of the game to have any chance of winning. Here are the nine basic rules for federal taxation of gambling. Don't worry if some (or all) of these rules seem confusing. They are explained in much more detail in later chapters, as referenced below.

### Rule #1: Gamblers Are Not Treated Fairly

Perhaps because gambling is viewed as "sinful," gamblers are treated very harshly by the tax laws. Indeed, in some cases gamblers are treated worse than criminals. Don't expect the rules discussed in this book to be fair, or even make sense.

### Rule #2: All Gambling Winnings Are Taxable Income

*All* gambling winnings are taxable income—that is, income

subject to both federal and state income taxes (except for the seven states that have no income taxes). It makes no difference how you earn your winnings—whether at a casino, gambling website, church raffle, or your friendly neighborhood poker game.

It also makes no difference *where* you win: whether at a casino or other gambling establishment in the United States (including those on Indian reservations), in a foreign country such as Mexico or Aruba, on a cruise ship, Mississippi river boat, or at a online casino hosted outside the U.S. As far as the IRS is concerned, a win is a win and must be included on your tax return.

Gambling winnings include not only the money you win, but the fair market value of any prizes or "comps" you receive as well. See Chapter 4.

### Rule #3: All Your Winnings Must Be Listed On Your Tax Return

If, like the vast majority of people, you're a recreational gambler, you're supposed to report *all* your gambling winnings on your tax return every year. You may not, repeat **NOT,** subtract your losses from your winnings and only report the amount left over, if any. *You're supposed to report every penny you win, even if your losses exceeded your winnings for the year.*

### Rule #4: Gambling Losses May Be Deducted Up to the Amount of Your Winnings

Fortunately, although you must list all your winnings on your tax return, you don't have to pay tax on the full amount. You are allowed to list your annual gambling losses as an itemized deduction on Schedule A of your tax return. If you lost as much as, or more than, you won during the year, your losses will offset your winnings. Even if you lost more than you won, you may only deduct as much as you won during the year.

However, you get no deduction for your losses at all if you don't itemize your deductions—just one of the ways gamblers are badly treated by the tax laws. (See Chapter 6.)

### Rule #5: Some Gambling Winnings Must Be Reported to the IRS By the House

Gambling is a cash business, so how will the IRS know how much you won during the year? Casinos, race tracks, state lotteries, bingo halls and other gambling establishments located in the United States are required to tell the IRS if you win more than a specified dollar amount. They do this by filing a tax form called Form W2-G with the IRS. You're given a copy of the form as well. When a W2-G must be filed depends on the type of game you play and how much you win. For example, the casino must file a W2-G if you win $1,200 or more playing slots; but only if you win $1,500 or more at keno. If you have one or more wins exceeding the reporting threshold, the IRS will know that you earned at least that much gambling income during the year. If this income is not listed on your tax return, you'll likely hear from the IRS. See Chapter 2.

### Rule #6 You Must Be Able to Prove the Amount of Your Wins and Losses

As the above rules should make clear, you must list both your total annual gambling winnings and losses on your tax return. If you're audited, your losses will be allowed by the IRS only if you can prove the amount of *both* your winnings and losses. You're supposed do this by keeping detailed records of all your gambling wins and losses during the year. This is where most gamblers slip up—they fail to keep adequate records (or any records at all). As a result, *you can end up owing taxes on your winnings even though your losses exceed your winnings for the year.* This has happened to many gamblers who failed to keep records.

Chapter 5 provides detailed guidance on how to keep records and what to do if you don't have any. *Proper record keeping is the single most important thing this book can teach you.*

### Rule #7: Winnings and Losses Are Determined by the Gambling Session

How do you figure out how much you won and lost during the year? You are not required to keep track of every single bet you make. Rather, you calculate your winnings and losses by the gambling session. A gambling session can be anything from a single bet at a slot machine to many days of consecutive play at a poker tournament. Chapter 4 explains this very important concept.

### Rule #8: The House Must Withhold Taxes From Some Gambling Winnings

It's not bad enough that the house must act as an IRS snitch. It may also have to serve as an unpaid bill collector for Uncle Sam. Depending on the game you play and how much you bet and win, the casino or other gambling establishment may be required to withhold 28% of your winnings and send them to the IRS. Such withholding is required, for example, if you more $1,200 or more on any one bet while playing slot machines. See Chapter 2.

### Rule #9: The Rules Differ for Professional Gamblers

If you gamble full-time to earn a living, you may qualify as a professional gambler for tax purposes. Professional gamblers inhabit a different tax universe than those who gamble for fun. In general, gambling pros are treated better by the IRS than amateurs, but few people qualify as gambling professionals. Refer to Chapter 8 to see if you make the grade, and how to deal with your taxes if you do.

##  Five Myths About Gambling Online

Millions of Americans gamble online for money. Online poker is particularly popular. There are several myths floating around about taxes on online gambling winnings. Don't engage in the wishful thinking behind these myths—it could get you into deep trouble with the IRS:

### Myth #1: When it comes to taxes, online gambling is different from other forms of gambling

As far as taxes are concerned, it makes absolutely no difference whether you gamble online or in a brick-and-mortar casino. All forms of gambling are treated exactly the same way—the way described in this book.

### Myth #2: You don't need to pay tax on winnings from offshore online casinos

All United States citizens must report and pay taxes on their gambling income from wherever they win it. It makes no difference whether you gamble in a casino physically located in the United States or in a foreign country, or through a website that is hosted in a foreign country. All that matters is that you win money from any form of gambling, which includes online poker.

### Myth #3: Internet gambling is illegal, so you'll get arrested if report online winnings

It's true that the FBI says that online gambling is illegal; and a few states, including Illinois, Indiana, Louisiana, South Dakota and Washington, have outlawed online gambling or some forms of it. However, it remains far from clear whether online gambling is really illegal in the United States. No federal law specifically says that online gambling is against the law. Moreover, even if it is illegal, you still have the legal duty to report and pay taxes on your winnings. If the IRS finds out that you won money from illegal gambling, it will not report you to other law enforcement agencies. But the IRS can prosecute you if you fail to pay taxes on your winnings—this is how Al Capone got sent to Alcatraz.

Note that while the legality of online gambling is unclear, it is against federal law for banks, credit card companies, payment processers like PayPal and Neteller, and other financial institutions to accept money transfers from or to online gambling accounts. But this law applies only to money transfers between financial institutions and online casinos, not to individuals who gamble online.

### Myth #4: No tax is due until you withdraw your money from offshore accounts

This is absolutely and utterly false. You owe tax on your gambling winnings as soon as they are made freely available to you—that is, deposited in an account that you can cash-out at any time. It makes no difference whether the money is in an account at an offshore online casino or actually in your pocket.

### Myth #5: The IRS will never know you gamble online

It's true that online gambling websites hosted in foreign countries need not, and do not, comply with the tax reporting rules that apply to United States casinos and other gambling establishments. Thus, they will not file form W-2G with the IRS when you win large jackpots.

However, this doesn't necessarily mean that IRS will never know that you've won money from online gambling. First of all, you may be legally required to report to the IRS that you have money in an account with an offshore casino—failure to comply with this requirement can have severe consequences. The existence of such offshore accounts will likely place you under increased IRS scrutiny. (See Chapter 2 for a detailed discussion of this issue.)

Moreover, if you're audited and the IRS discovers large sums of money you can't account for, you'll have some explaining to do. It is also possible that some time in the future the IRS will obtain financial records from online gambling websites or payment processors.

# What Does the IRS Know and When Does It Know It?

Every gambler needs to understand that casinos and other gambling establishments based in the United States are required by law to act as IRS snitches. If you win more than a threshold amount, the casino is required to file a form with the IRS reporting how much you won. Moreover, even if you don't win any money, the casino may have to report to the IRS if you engage in any large cash transactions with the casino.

Whether your winnings must be reported to the IRS by a casino depends on the type of game you play and how much you win. Of course, *you are legally required to report all your gambling income on your tax return, whether or not the casino or other gambling establishment files a tax form with the IRS reporting your winnings.*

IRS computers automatically check whether gambling establishments have filed any of the forms discussed below reporting that you won a specified amount of money. If you don't include all your reported winnings on your return, you'll likely receive an IRS deficiency notice demanding that you pay taxes on the unreported income. This is how the vast majority of gamblers get into trouble with the IRS.

There are three different tax forms that are filed with the IRS to report gambling winnings. It makes no practical difference to you which of these forms are sent to the IRS. But there are important differences as to when these forms must be sent to the IRS by gambling establishments.

##  Retired Couple Snitched On by Casinos

Ira and Paula Lutz were a retired couple who played slots and video poker at the casinos in Biloxi, Mississippi two or three times a week. They had a few nice wins during the year; but, even though they didn't keep any records of their wins and losses, they were certain that they lost more than they won. They reported no gambling income on their 1996 tax return. Three years later the Lutz's opened their mail and found an IRS deficiency notice claiming that they had $91,000 in unreported gambling income for 1996 on which they owed income tax. How did the IRS come up with the number $91,000? It got the information from the casinos where the Lutz's gambled. The four casinos at which the couple did the bulk of their gambling sent the IRS a total of 18 tax forms reporting that the Lutz's had won the money. Because the Lutz's couldn't prove exactly how much they had lost gambling during 1996 they had to pay taxes on part of these winnings.

# IRS Form W2-G

The main form used to report gambling winnings to the IRS is form W2-G, *Certain Gambling Winnings* (G stands for gambling). This is an "information return" used just for gambling. (An information return is filed to inform the IRS how much money a taxpayer earns in certain types of transactions.) The IRS receives nearly 5 million Form W2-Gs each year. Here is a copy of the first page of the form:

| 3232 | ☐ CORRECTED | | OMB No. 1545-0238 |
|------|-------------|--|--------------------|
| PAYER'S name | 1 Gross winnings | 2 Federal income tax withheld | **2011** |
| Street address | 3 Type of wager | 4 Date won | Form W-2G |
| City, state, and ZIP code | 5 Transaction | 6 Race | Certain Gambling Winnings |
| Federal identification number    Telephone number | 7 Winnings from identical wagers | 8 Cashier | For Privacy Act and Paperwork Reduction Act Notice, see the 2011 General Instructions for Certain Information Returns. |
| WINNER'S name | 9 Winner's taxpayer identification no. | 10 Window | |
| Street address (including apt. no.) | 11 First I.D. | 12 Second I.D. | |
| City, state, and ZIP code | 13 State/Payer's state identification no. | 14 State income tax withheld | File with Form 1096. |
| Under penalties of perjury, I declare that, to the best of my knowledge and belief, the name, address, and taxpayer identification number that I have furnished correctly identify me as the recipient of this payment and any payments from identical wagers, and that no other person is entitled to any part of these payments. | | | Copy A For Internal Revenue Service Center |
| Signature ▶ | | Date ▶ | |
| Form W-2G | Cat. No. 10138V | Department of the Treasury - Internal Revenue Service | |

As you can see, the form must include the amount of your winnings and any tax withheld from them. The casino or other gambling establishment will require you to furnish your name, address, and Social Security number or other taxpayer identification number so that this information can be included on the form. The casino is also supposed to verify this information with two forms of identification. This can be your driver's license, Social Security card, voter registration card, or other proper identification. If you lack proper identification, the casino can't complete the form and is not allowed to pay you your winnings. If you don't have your ID with you, you can ask the casino to hold your winnings for you so you can come back later with your ID.

If you fail to provide your Social Security number, the casino or other gambling establishment is required to withhold 28% of your winnings and pay them directly to the IRS. This is called backup withholding (see Chapter 3). You don't need to have your Social Security card with you; but, if you don't, you must know your number and complete an IRS W9 Form testifying to your correct number. It will be much easier and faster if you have your Social Security card with you.

Form W-2G is a multi-part form, copies will be sent to the IRS and your state tax department. You get three copies: one to keep for your records, one to attach to your state tax return (if necessary), and one to file with your federal tax return (required only if tax is withheld from your winnings). The casino or other gambling establishment must send your copies of Form W-2G to you by January 31 of the year following the year you won the amount.

These rules apply to casinos, race tracks, dog tracks, state-run lotteries, sweepstakes, jai lai operators, and bingo parlors. Even churches and other nonprofit organizations may have to follow these rules if they hold bingo games, raffles, or other gambling events to raise money.

A Form W-2G must be filed only if you win more than a threshold amount—the amounts vary according to the type of gambling involved. It's a good idea to become familiar with these thresholds.

### Slot machines

A form W-2G must be filed only if you win $1,200 or more from a slot machine on *a single spin or hand*. Multiple spins or hands are not added together. If you play a multi-line machine, the amounts you win on all the lines are added together to determine your total win. The amount you bet is not deducted from your winnings to determine whether you pass the $1,200 threshold. To avoid having to file a tax form, some slot machines are designed to pay out no more than $1,119 on any single bet.

If you win $1,200 or more, you will be paid by hand by a casino employee. A light will flash or bell will go off and a casino employee will ask you to provide the necessary information to complete the Form W-2G.

#  Form W-2G Session Logs

If you play high stakes machines ($50 a hand or more), you could easily win many $1,200+ jackpots during a gambling session. Having to stop play and fill out a Form W-2G every time this happens would slow down play considerably. To avoid this, casinos can keep track of how much you win during the session and then issue you one Form W-2G with the total. This is called being put "on session" or "on the board."

## Video poker

Video poker winnings are treated the same way as slot machine winnings.

## Poker tournaments

If you enter a poker tournament, the sponsor must file a Form W2-G if you win more than $5,000 ($5,000.01 or more) after deducting your entry or "buy-in" fee. For example, if you enter a tournament for $1,000 and end up winning $6,000.01, the tournament sponsor must file Form W2-G. This rule came into effect on March 4, 2008. Winnings earned before that date did not have to be reported.

## Bingo

The rules for bingo are the same as for slot machines—a W-2G must be filed if you win $1,200 or more from a single game.

## Keno

A W2-G need be filed only if you win $1,500 or more from keno, *less the amount of your wager*. For example, if you bet $10 and win $1,500, your winnings for IRS purposes are $1,490 ($1,500$10 = $1,490). Video keno, however, is considered to be the same as a slot machine. Thus, it has the $1,200 reporting threshold, not counting the amount of the wager.

## All other games

For all other games, no matter what type of game you play or bet you make, a WG-2 must be filed only if:

- you win $600 or more on a single bet, hand, or play, *and*
- your winnings are at least 300 times the amount you bet.

For example, if you bet $2 on the daily double at your local race track and win $700, the track will have to file a Form W-2G—your $700 win exceeds both the $600 and 300 x bet thresholds. But if you bet $3 at the track and win $700, no W-2G need be filed since your win is only 234 times the amount of your bet.

In determining whether the $600 threshold is passed, the gambling establishment may reduce the winnings by the amount of the wager—however, it is not required to do so. For example, if you bet $2 at the track and win $600, a W2-G must be filed by the track if it doesn't deduct the amount of the wager. On the other hand, if the track deducts the amount of your wager, your winnings are only $598 and need not be reported.

Of course, it's not very common for a gambler to win 300 times the amount he or she bets at a casino table games such as blackjack, craps, roulette, or baccarat. Thus, Form W-2Gs are rarely filed for winners of table games—one of the advantages of playing these games. For example, if you bet $1,000 at a hand of blackjack and win, you'll double your money. Although your $1,000 winnings exceed the $600 threshold, they are not 300 times the amount you bet, and no W2-G need be filed. Likewise, if you bet $100 on a number on the roulette wheel and win, you'll get $3,500—only 35 times the amount you bet. Again, no W2-G need be filed. About the only time W2-Gs are filed for table game players is when they win big on some poker progressives and royal/straight flushes.

A win 300 or more times your bet is most likely to occur at the race track, dog track, sports betting, lottery, bingo games, sweepstakes, or raffles.

| IRS Reporting Requirements for Gambling Winnings | | |
|---|---|---|
| **Type of Game** | **Winnings at Least:** | **Reduced by Amount of Bet?** |
| Slot machines | $1,200 | No |
| Poker tournaments | $5,000.01 | Yes |
| Keno | $1,500 | Yes |
| Bingo | $1,200 | No |
| All other games—for example, casino table games, raffles, rack track betting | $600 and at least 300 times amount bet | At option of gambling establishment |

## IRS Form 1099-MISC

IRS Form 1099-MISC is another type of information return. It is not used just for gambling. Rather, it must be filed when many different types of businesses pay more than $600 to someone in the course of a year. Ordinarily, casinos and other gambling establishments will send you a Form 1099 only when you win more than $600 *without making a wager.*

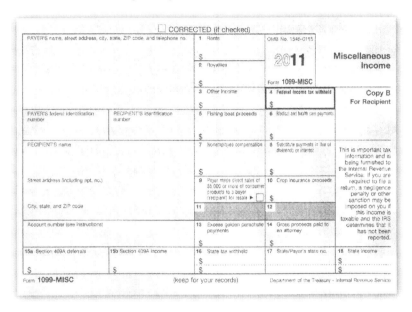

### Prizes

If you win a non-cash prize worth $600 or more without making a wager, the fair market value of the prize must be reported to the IRS on Form 1099-MISC. For example, if you win a car in a casino drawing, the casino will file a Form 1099-MISC with the IRS reporting the cash value of the car.

## What is fair market value?

Disputes can easily arise as to the fair market value of a prize. For example, how much is a new car worth? The basic rule is that "fair market value" is the amount that would induce a willing and able buyer to buy, and a willing seller to sell, neither being under special pressure to buy or sell. Whether you should use the retail value or wholesale or discounted value of a prize is unclear. Often, casinos will report the value as the item's list or retail price. However, the retail or list price may not really be an item's true fair market value. For example, the fair market value of a new car is typically less than its list price. If you can prove that the item is actually worth less than reported to the IRS by the casino, you can use the lesser amount. Attach a note to your return explaining why you used the lower value.

## Comps and gifts

Casinos and other gambling establishments typically give gamblers "comps" (short for complimentaries) to encourage them to keep playing. In the case of brick-and-mortar casinos, these can include free drinks, rooms, meals, or shows. Both brick-and-mortar and online casinos also usually have frequent player programs in which players earn frequent player points (FPPs) depending on how much they gamble. FPPs can be cashed in for merchandise, entries into poker tournaments, or cash. Bonuses are another type of comp—these may consist of a credit that can only be used to gamble in the casino (called free play), or they can be in cash. Online poker rooms also often refund to players a portion of the rake they collect on each hand—termed rakeback.

The basic rule is that all comps must be treated exactly the same as gambling winnings. This means that you are supposed to add their fair market value to your winnings for tax purposes.

If a United States-based casino gives you comps worth $600 or more over the course of a year, it is supposed to file a 1099-MISC form reporting the amount to the IRS. However, comps are not consistently reported to the IRS by casinos and other gambling establishments—for example, the value of small comps such as free drinks and meals is not counted toward the $600 limit. Large comps—for example, a comp for $1,000 per night hotel room—are ordinarily reported. Online casinos located outside the United States are not required to file Form 1099 with the IRS reporting the value of their comps.

Some types of comps can present complications which have not been addressed by the IRS. Consider Frequent Player Points. For example, if you cash in your FPPs to obtain merchandise worth $500, it's clear that you would add the $500 to your winnings for the year. Likewise, if you exchange your points for cash, you'd add the amount to your winnings (FPPs are typically worth about 1.5 cents per point). But what if you have unused FPPs in your casino account at the end of the year? Do you include them in your winnings? The conservative approach would be to value your unused FPPs at the end of the year by their cash value and add the amount to your winnings.

Free play can be treated differently than FPPs because it ordinarily has a expiration date—if you don't take advantage of your free play by a certain date you lose it. In contrast, FPPs can be cashed in any time. Thus, the fact that you have accrued free play at the end of the year doesn't necessarily mean you'll ever use it. For this reason, it makes sense to treat the value of free play as winnings only when you actually use it.

##  Whale Loses at Casino, Wins In Court

Robert Libutti was a rich man and a big gambler. Over a three-year period he lost over $8 million at the Trump Casino in Atlantic City. To encourage his gambling habit, the casino gave him comps that included five Rolls-Royces, three Ferraris, European vacations, Rolex watches and other jewelry, fine Champagne, and tickets to major sporting events. These comps amounted to $443,000 in 1987, $974,000 in 1988, and $1.1 million in 1989. The casino reported the value of the comps to the IRS on Form 1099-MISC. On his returns for these years, Libutti included the comps in his gross income, and deducted gambling losses up to the amount of the comps. The IRS disallowed these deductions, claiming that comps were not gambling winnings. Fortunately for all gamblers, Libutti appealed the IRS's decision in court. The court found that the comps were gambling winnings—gains from wagering. Thus, Libutti was allowed to deduct $2.5 million of his gambling winnings from his comp income—meaning it was effectively tax free. You can do the same. (*Libutti v. Comm'r*, TCM 1996-108.)

## Multiple Winners—Form 5754

It's not uncommon for people to pool their money to gamble. For example, two or more people may buy lottery tickets together. If you're a member of such a betting pool, you should have the gambling establishment file multiple W-2G forms listing each individual's share of the pot. To do this, you must complete and give to the gambling establishment IRS Form 5754, *Statement by Person(s) Receiving Gambling Winnings.*

You list on this form the names, addresses, and Social Security numbers for each person in the pool. You also indicate each person's share of the winnings. If regular gambling withholding is required, the form must be signed and dated by the person receiving the winnings.

| Form **5754** | Statement by Person(s) Receiving Gambling Winnings | | |
|---|---|---|---|
| (Rev. December 2008) | ► Recipients of gambling winnings should see the instructions on the back of this form. | | OMB No. 1545-0239 |
| Department of the Treasury Internal Revenue Service | ► Payers of gambling winnings should see the separate Instructions for Forms W-2G and 5754. | | Return to payer. Do not send to the IRS. |
| Date won | Type of winnings | Game number | Machine number | Race number |

**Part I** Person to Whom Winnings Are Paid

| Name | | Address | |
|---|---|---|---|
| Taxpayer identification number | Other I.D. | Amount received | Federal income tax withheld |

**Part II** Persons to Whom Winnings Are Taxable *(continued on page 2)*

| (a) Name | (b) Taxpayer identification number | (c) Address | (d) Amount won | (e) Winnings from identical wagers |
|---|---|---|---|---|
| | | | | |
| | | | | |
| | | | | |
| | | | | |
| | | | | |
| | | | | |
| | | | | |
| | | | | |
| | | | | |

Under penalties of perjury, I declare that, to the best of my knowledge and belief, the names, addresses, and taxpayer identification numbers that I have furnished correctly identify me as the recipient of this payment and correctly identify each person entitled to any part of this payment and any payments from identical wagers.

Signature ►                                             Date ►

For Paperwork Reduction Act Notice, see back of form.          Cat. No. 12100R          Form **5754** (Rev. 12-2008)

## Other Ways the IRS Can Learn About Your Gambling Activities

The main way the IRS learns about your gambling winnings is through the filing of Forms W2-G and 1099-MISC by casinos and other gambling establishments. However, there are other forms that may have to be filed with the IRS by casinos, even if you don't win any money. Moreover, you may be required to report yourself to the IRS if you have foreign financial accounts.

These forms are not specifically intended to track the amount of your gambling winnings. However, they can indicate that you have won money and serve as a useful audit lead for the IRS.

### Casino currency transaction reports

The IRS can learn about your gambling activity through currency transaction reports of large cash transactions. Casinos and card clubs located in the United States with gross annual revenues over $1 million must follow much the same cash reporting rules as banks and other financial institutions. Indian casinos must also comply. These laws are intended to prevent money laundering by criminals and terrorists, and tax evasion.

Casinos must file with the IRS Form 103, Currency Transactions Report By Casinos and Card Clubs (CTRC), whenever you engage in cash transactions involving more than $10,000 in a single gaming day. The casino must also obtain adequate identification from you, such as a Social Security number, driver's license, or other government issued identification.

It makes no difference if the money is paid to the casino (Cash In), or paid out to you (Cash Out). Your Cash In and Cash Out totals for the day must be kept separate. Thus, a CTRC will be filed if you use cash to purchase more than $10,000 in chips or credit at the cage, bet or win more than $10,000 on any single bet on table games, or withdraw more than $10,000 from the casino. Cash-in includes front money or safekeeping deposits as well as chip purchases in the pit.

*EXAMPLE: Jack, a regular at the Lady Luck Casino, purchases $11,000 in chips with cash and starts playing blackjack. He never bets more than $100 at a time or wins more than $1,000 on any single bet. After he finishes gambling for the day he cashes in his chips and receives $18,000 in cash from the casino. The casino must file a CTRC reporting $11,000 Cash In and $18,000 Cash Out.*

However, casinos do not have to report the following types of transactions:

- jackpots from slot machines or video lottery terminals
- bills inserted into electronic slot machines and other electronic gaming devices in multiple transactions
- cash ins when the money cashed in is the same physical currency previously wagered in a money play on the same table game without leaving the table, or
- cash outs won in a money play when the money is the same physical currency wagered (however, when a customer increases a subsequent cash bet (money play), at the same

table game without departing, the increase in the amount of the currency bet is considered a new bet of currency and therefore a reportable transaction in currency).

People sometimes try to avoid being reported to the government by breaking up their transactions into multiple amounts that are all less than $10,000. This is called "structuring" and is illegal. It also usually doesn't work. Multiple currency transactions must be treated as a single transaction if the casino knows that: (1) they are made by or on behalf of the same person, and (2) they result in either cash in or cash out by the casino totaling more than $10,000 during any one normal business day.

*EXAMPLE: During a single day, Jack from the above example plays blackjack, craps, and baccarat. He bets no more than $1,000 at any one time and never wins or loses more than $3,000 on any single bet. At the end of the day Jack has won a total of $13,000 from all his gambling activities. Because of the anti-structuring rule, his multiple transactions must be treated as a single transaction, and the casino is required to file a CRTC for Jack's transactions for the day.*

Casinos use their computer systems to keep track of all your pit buy-ins and casino cage transactions. If your daily total cash in or cash out exceeds the $10,000 limit, they will file a CTRC.

### Suspicious activity reporting by casinos

There is another form that a casino may file about you without you ever even knowing about it. This is the "Suspicious Activity Report for Casinos and Card Clubs" ("SARC," FinCEN Form 102). Federal law requires casinos and card clubs to file a SARC for every transaction or group of related transactions totaling $5,000 or more whenever the casino knows or suspects that a customer is trying to avoid the filing of a Currency Transaction Report for Casinos (CTRC), or involves funds derived from illegal activities. SARCs are also supposed to be filed if a casino customer behaves suspiciously—that is, engages in transactions that are out of the ordinary.

Some things that you could do that might be considered suspicious are:

- exchanging many small bills for large ones
- exchanging several monetary instruments, such as traveler's checks, for one casino check
- regularly conducting currency transactions that are just below $10,000
- purchasing chips and then, after minimal gambling, redeeming the chips for a check
- using other casino patrons to cash-out chips
- supplying other patrons with cash to purchase chips
- using the casino purely for its financial services, or
- using identification that appears to be altered or forged.

Unlike Currency Transaction Reports, which must be filed only for transactions involving cash, SARCs must be filed whether cash or other forms of money are involved, such as checks.

The casino is not allowed to tell you that it filed a SARC about you, and will not give you a copy of the form.

### Your duty to report foreign bank accounts over $10,000

Casinos located outside the United States are not required to comply with any of the IRS's reporting rules. Thus, if you gamble on the Internet with offshore casinos, they will not report your winnings to the IRS on Forms W2-G or 1099-MISC, or file any currency transaction reports. However, you may be legally required to report to the IRS if you have a financial account with an offshore casino.

A United States citizen must file a Foreign Bank Account Report (FBAR, Form TD F 90-22.1) with the IRS whenever he or she has an interest in, or signature authority over, a foreign financial account with a value over $10,000 any time during the calendar year. It makes no difference if the average amount in the account during the year is less than $10,000 or all the money is withdrawn by the end of the year. If the account held more than $10,000 any time during the year, the FBAR must be filed.

The IRS has ruled that these requirements apply to accounts with offshore casinos. Thus, for example, a U.S. citizen who wires or otherwise deposits $15,000 with poker.net, located in the Isle of Man, is subject to the reporting requirement, even if he or she promptly loses money and the account never again has a value over $10,000.

##  Frequent Player Points

The FBAR filing requirement is not limited to foreign accounts containing cash. You're also supposed to file an FBAR if a foreign account has non-monetary assets of more than $10,000. For example, the cash surrender value of a life insurance policy is such a non-monetary assets. For this reason, if the cash value of your frequent player points at an offshore casino account exceeds $10,000 any time during the year, you should file an FBAR.

The penalties for failing to file FBARs are severe. There is a minimum $10,000 penalty if your failure to file was inadvertent. However, if you are found guilty of willfully not filing an FBAR, the minimum fine is $100,000 or half the value of the account, whichever is greater.

The FBAR must contain the name and address of each casino in which you hold an account over $10,000, the account number(s) and the maximum amount in the account during the year. The form is not filed with your tax return. Instead, it must be separately filed with the IRS by June 30 each year—in this case, filed means received by the IRS, not placed in the mail. For a copy of the FBAR form and detailed guidance on filing, review the FAQs on the IRS website at http://www.irs.gov/businesses/small/article/0,,id=210244,00.html

Offshore Casino Addresses

If you are required to file an FBAR form, you are supposed to provide the mailing addresses of the casinos or other sites with whom you have foreign accounts. Some offshore casinos keep their addresses secret. Thus, it may be impossible for you to provide this information. However, accountant and poker expert Russ Fox has compiled a list of addresses for many online poker and gambling sites at: http://www. taxabletalk.com/2009/03/10/online-gambling-addresses/

# Gambling Establishments Exempt From the IRS Reporting Requirements

The IRS reporting requirements apply to gambling establishments physically located within the United States. Thus, for example, they don't apply if you gamble in a foreign country. Internet gambling websites hosted outside the U.S. also need not comply with the rules. Likewise, the rules shouldn't apply if you gamble on a foreign-registered cruise ship in international waters. However, some cruise lines follow the reporting rules anyway. For example, Carnival Cruise Lines does so for passengers who are U.S. citizens or permanent residents (see http://www.oceanplayersclub.com/AboutTheClub/FAQ.aspx). If you intend to do heavy gambling on a cruise, you may wish to check to see what their policy is on reporting winnings to the IRS.

**TD F 90-22.1**
(Rev. October 2008)
Department of the Treasury

Do not use previous editions of this form after December 31, 2008

## REPORT OF FOREIGN BANK AND FINANCIAL ACCOUNTS

Do NOT file with your Federal Tax Return

OMB No. 1545-2038

1 This Report is for Calendar Year Ended 12/31

Amended ☐

### Part I  Filer Information

2 Type of Filer

a ☐ Individual  b ☐ Partnership  c ☐ Corporation  d ☐ Consolidated  e ☐ Fiduciary or Other—Enter type _____

| 3 U.S. Taxpayer Identification Number | 4 Foreign identification (Complete only if Item 3 is not applicable.) | | 5 Individual's Date of Birth MM/DD/YYYY |
|---|---|---|---|
| | a Type: ☐ Passport  ☐ Other _____ | | |
| If filer has no U.S. Identification Number complete Item 4. | b Number _____ | c Country of Issue _____ | |
| 6 Last Name or Organization Name | 7 First Name | | 8 Middle Initial |

9 Address (Number, Street, and Apt. or Suite No.)

| 10 City | 11 State | 12 Zip/Postal Code | 13 Country |
|---|---|---|---|

14 Does the filer have a financial interest in 25 or more financial accounts?

☐ Yes  If "Yes" enter total number of accounts _____

(If "Yes" is checked, do not complete Part II or Part III, but retain records of this information)

☐ No

### Part II  Information on Financial Account(s) Owned Separately

| 15 Maximum value of account during calendar year reported | 16 Type of account  a ☐ Bank  b ☐ Securities  c ☐ Other—Enter type below |
|---|---|

17 Name of Financial Institution in which account is held

| 18 Account number or other designation | 19 Mailing Address (Number, Street, Suite Number) of financial institution in which account is held |
|---|---|

| 20 City | 21 State, if known | 22 Zip/Postal Code, if known | 23 Country |
|---|---|---|---|

### Signature

| 44 Filer Signature | 45 Filer Title, if not reporting a personal account | 46 Date (MM/DD/YYYY) |
|---|---|---|

File this form with: U.S. Department of the Treasury, P.O. Box 32621, Detroit, MI 48232-0621

This form should be used to report a financial interest in, signature authority, or other authority over one or more financial accounts in foreign countries, as required by the Department of the Treasury Regulations (31 CFR 103). No report is required if the aggregate value of the accounts did not exceed $10,000. **See Instructions For Definitions.**

### PRIVACY ACT AND PAPERWORK REDUCTION ACT NOTICE

Pursuant to the requirements of Public Law 93-579 (Privacy Act of 1974), notice is hereby given that the authority to collect information on TD F 90-22.1 in accordance with 5 USC 552a (e) is Public Law 91-508; 31 USC 5314; 5 USC 301; 31 CFR 103.

The principal purpose for collecting the information is to assure maintenance of reports where such reports or records have a high degree of usefulness in criminal, tax, or regulatory investigations or proceedings. The information collected may be provided to those officers and employees of any constituent unit of the Department of the Treasury who have a need for the records in the performance of their duties. The records may be referred to any other department or agency of the United States upon the request of the head of such department or agency for use in a criminal, tax, or regulatory investigation or proceeding. The information collected may also be provided to appropriate state, local, and foreign law enforcement and regulatory personnel in the performance of their official duties. Disclosure of this information is mandatory. Civil and criminal penalties, including in certain circumstances a fine of not more than $500,000 and imprisonment of not more than five years, are provided for failure to file a report, supply information, and for filing a false or fraudulent report. Disclosure of the Social Security number is mandatory. The authority to collect is 31 CFR 103. The Social Security number will be used as a means to identify the individual who files the report.

The estimated average burden associated with this collection of information is 20 minutes per respondent or record keeper, depending on individual circumstances. Comments regarding the accuracy of this burden estimate, and suggestions for reducing the burden should be directed to the Internal Revenue Service, Bank Secrecy Act Policy, 5000 Ellin Road C-3-242, Lanham MD 20706.

Cat No. 12996D                    Form **TD F 90-22.1** (Rev. 10-2008)

**FinCEN**
**Form 102**
April 2003
Previous editions will not be
accepted after December 31, 2003

**Suspicious Activity Report**
**by Casinos and Card Clubs**

▶ Please type or print. Always complete entire report. Items
marked with an asterisk * are considered critical (see instructions).

OMB No. 1506-0006

1 Check the box if this report corrects a prior report (see instructions on page 6) ☐

## Part I  Subject Information

2 Check box (a) ☐ if more than one subject  box (b) ☐ subject information unavailable

*3 Individual's last name or entity's full name

*4 First name

5 Middle initial

6 also known as (AKA- individual), doing business as (DBA- entity)

7 Occupation / type of business

*8 Address

*9 City

*10 State | *11 ZIP code | *12 Country (if not U.S.) | 13 Vehicle license # / state (optional) a. number | b. state

*14 SSN / ITIN (individual) or EIN (entity) | *15 Account number  No account affected ☐ | Account open ? Yes ☐  No ☐ | 16 Date of birth  MM DD YYYY

*17 Government issued identification (if available)  a ☐ Driver's license/state ID  b ☐ Passport  d ☐ Alien registration
d ☐ Other _____
e Number: _____  f  Issuing state or country _____

18 Phone number - work  (   )   -   | 19 Phone number - home  (   )   -   | 20 E-mail address (if available)

21 Affiliation or relationship to casino/card club
a ☐ Customer  b ☐ Agent  c ☐ Junket / tour operator  d ☐ Employee  e ☐ Check cashing operator
f ☐ Supplier  g ☐ Concessionaire  h ☐ Other (Explain in Part VI)

22 Does casino/card club still have a business association and/or an employee/employer relationship with suspect?
a ☐ Yes  b ☐ No  If no , why?  c ☐ Barred  d ☐ Resigned  e ☐ Terminated  f ☐ Other (Specify in Part VI) | 23 Date action taken(22)  MM DD YYYY

## Part II  Suspicious Activity Information

*24 Date or date range of suspicious activity
From  __/__/__  MM DD YYYY  To  __/__/__  MM DD YYYY | *25 Total dollar amount involved in suspicious activity  $           .00

* 26 Type of suspicious activity:
a ☐ Bribery/gratuity
b ☐ Check fraud (includes counterfeit)
c ☐ Credit/debit card fraud (incl. counterfeit)
d ☐ Embezzlement/theft
e ☐ Large currency exchange(s)
f ☐ Minimal gaming with large transactions
g ☐ Misuse of position
h ☐ Money laundering
i ☐ No apparent business or lawful purpose
j ☐ Structuring
k ☐ Unusual use of negotiable instruments (checks)
l ☐ Use of multiple credit or deposit accounts
m ☐ Unusual use of wire transfers
n ☐ Unusual use of counter checks or markers
o ☐ False or conflicting ID(s)
p ☐ Terrorist financing
q ☐ Other (Describe in Part VI)

## Part III  Law Enforcement or Regulatory Contact Information

27 If law enforcement or a regulatory agency has been contacted (excluding submission of a SARC), check the appropriate box.
a ☐ DEA
b ☐ U.S. Attorney (** 28)
c ☐ IRS
d ☐ FBI
e ☐ U.S. Customs Service
f ☐ U.S. Secret Service
g ☐ Local law enforcement
h ☐ State gaming commission
i ☐ State law enforcement
j ☐ Tribal gaming commission
k ☐ Tribal law enforcement
l ☐ Other (List in item 28)

28 Other authority contacted (for box 27 g through l) ** List U.S. Attorney office here.

29 Name of person contacted (for all of box 27)

30 Telephone number of individual contacted in box 29  (   )   -   | 31 Date Contacted  __/__/__  MM DD YYYY

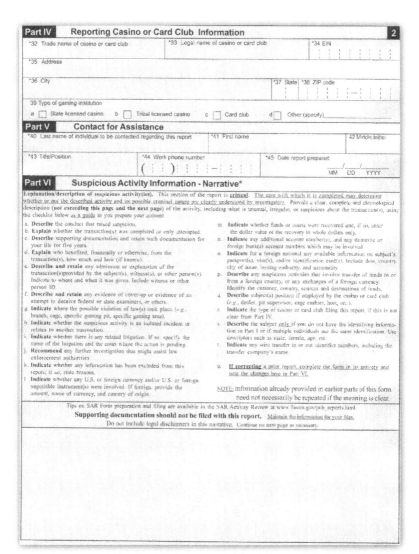

# Tax Withholding From Your Winnings

The previous chapter explained when casinos and other gambling establishments are required to report your gambling winnings to the IRS. This might seem bad enough, but it gets even worse. In some cases, casinos and other gambling establishments must also withhold income tax from your winnings. In effect, casinos are required to act as IRS tax collectors.

If you've ever been an employee, you already know about income tax withholding—your employer deducts the amount of your income taxes from your paycheck and pays the money to the IRS. Gambling tax withholding works much the same way. The casino or other gambling establishment deducts a percentage of your winnings and pays them directly to the IRS.

There are two types of withholding on gambling winnings: regular withholding at 28% (25% in 2010 and earlier), and backup withholding at 28%. Regular withholding is mandatory. Backup withholding is required only if you don't provide your Social Security number to the casino when it issues you a W-2G form. If a payment is already subject to regular gambling withholding, it is not subject to backup withholding.

All taxes withheld from winnings (whether regular or backup withholding) must be listed on the Form W-2G the casino or other gambling establishment files with the IRS to report the winnings. See Chapter 2 for more information about Form W-2G. You'll receive a copy of the form as well, and should include the amount in the total taxes withheld listed on your tax return.

##  Over-Withholding Is Common

It is very common for more tax to be withheld from your winnings than you actually end up owing at the end of the year. This is because withholding is based on your winnings on any single bet, not on the amount you win or lose during an entire gambling session. Moreover, you are not allowed to deduct your losses from your winnings for withholding purposes. If you win a substantial bet, have tax withheld, and then end up losing all the winnings during the same session, you don't get back the withheld amount from the casino. If more tax is withheld than you owe, you'll have to claim a refund on your tax return. In effect, you're giving a tax-free loan to the IRS.

# Regular Income Tax Withholding

Whether regular income tax withholding is required depends on the game you play and how much you bet and win. If regular withholding is required, the casino or other gambling establishment will withhold 28% from your net winnings—that is, 28% of your winnings minus the amount wagered (for 2010 and earlier the percentage is 25%). You will also be required to sign IRS Form W-2G. By signing, you declare that no other person is entitled to any portion of the payment and that the winnings are subject to regular gambling withholding.

### Table games, sports betting, horse racing, and most other types of gambling

Regular withholding is required for casino table games, sports betting, horse racing, dog racing, jai lai and any other games not discussed below only if:

- you win more than $5,000 (after subtracting the amount wagered), *and*
- your net winnings are at least 300 times more than you bet.

*EXAMPLE: Manny goes to the track and bets $2 on the Pick Six. He ends up winning $6,000. His net winnings are $5,598. This is more than $5,000 and more than 300 times his $2 bet. This* *means that the track must withhold 28% from his $5,998 in net winnings—$1,679.*

For multiple wagers sold on one ticket, each bet is considered separately for purposes of computing withholding. For example, if you make a $18 box bet on a Big Triple or Trifecta, the wager is considered to be nine $2 bets and not one $18 bet for withholding purposes. Thus, federal income tax must be withheld if you win $5,000 on a $18 box bet. In the eyes of the IRS, you've won the $5,000 on a single $2 bet, which is more than 300 times the amount you bet. If the box bet was counted as one $18 bet, no withholding would be required because $5,000 is less than 300 times $18.

One way you might try to avoid having your winnings reported to the IRS is to make multiple identical wagers on the same race, so that the amount won on any single ticket is less than $5,000. Unfortunately, the IRS has thought of this trick. To prevent it from working, it requires all winnings from identical wagers (for example, two $2 bets on a single horse to win the same race) be added together to determine if the total amount won from identical wagers is more than $5,000.

### Lotteries, sweepstakes, wagering pools

Regular withholding is required if your net winnings (total winnings minus amount bet) from a lottery, sweepstakes, raffle, or wagering pool are more than $5,000. These rules apply to state lotteries, church raffles, and charity drawings. If you make one wager for multiple raffle tickets, such as five tickets for $1, the wager is considered to be $.20 for each ticket.

*EXAMPLE: Lionel goes to a church raffle and buys a $1 ticket. At the drawing, his number is drawn and he wins $6,000. Because the proceeds from the wager are $5,999 ($6,000 prize minus $1 ticket) which is more than $5,000, the church must withhold $1,680 ($5,999 x 28%) from Lionel's winnings.*

### Poker tournaments

Regular withholding on poker tournament winnings is not necessary unless the tournament sponsor fails to file a Form W-2G when required. Form W-2G must be filed if you win more than $5,000, reduced by the amount of the entrance fee. If the sponsor fails to file the form, the IRS can require the sponsor to pay withholding out of its own pocket. To help them comply with these requirements, tournament sponsors are supposed to obtain the Social Security numbers of the tournament players. If you refuse to provide your Social Security number, the tournament sponsor must do backup withholding (see below).

### Slot Machines, bingo, keno

Regular withholding is not required no matter how much you win at slot machines, bingo, or keno. This is one advantage of playing these games.

### Noncash payments

What happens if you win a noncash prize or payment such as a car or vacation? Unfortunately, you can't escape withholding. Regular withholding is required on all noncash prizes with a fair market value over $5,000 after deducting the amount of the wager. For example, if you win a $50,000 car on a $10 raffle ticket, regular withholding will be required on $49,990.

There are two ways to do regular withholding on noncash payments: You can pay it out of your own pocket or the casino or other gambling establishment can pay it.

If you pay the withholding tax yourself, only 28% need be withheld (25% in 2010 and earlier). You pay the money to the casino or other gambling establishment which in turns pays it to the IRS.

If the casino or other gambling establishment pays the withholding tax itself, the withholding amount is 33.33%. The withholding percentage in this case is higher, because you get not only the value of the prize but also the value of having the taxes paid by the casino.

## Multiple winners

What happens if there are multiple winners on the same wager—for example, two or more people purchase a single winning lottery ticket? In this event, the total amount of the winnings (minus the amount wagered) is used to determine whether the withholding thresholds have been reached.

*EXAMPLE: Ed and Sally each chip in 50 cents to purchase a $1 lottery ticket and agree to split any winnings evenly. The ticket wins $5,002. The total net winnings are $5,001($5,002$1 = $5,001). Since this is more than the $5,000 withholding threshold for lottery winnings, 28% of $5,001 must be withheld from Ed and Sally's winnings. A separate Form W-2G is filed for each by the state lottery commission.*

## Backup Withholding

If a casino or other gambling establishment is required to file a Form W-2G reporting the amount of your winnings, it is supposed to obtain your taxpayer identification number (usually your Social Security number) and include it on the form. If you refuse to provide your number, the casino is required to withhold 28% from your winnings. This is called back-up withholding.

The IRS believes (probably rightly) that anyone who refuses to provide his or her taxpayer ID number will likely not voluntarily pay any tax on gambling winnings. Thus, backup withholding serves as a way for the IRS to make these people pay all or part of their gambling taxes in advance. If they end up paying too much, they'll have to claim a refund on their tax return for the year.

The general rule is that backup withholding is required only if:

- the casino or other gambling establishment has not already done regular withholding from your winnings, and
- you fail to furnish a correct taxpayer identification number (usually your Social Security number) to the casino, and
- your winnings are at least (1) $600, and (2) 300 times the amount of the wager.

However, if you fail to furnish your taxpayer ID, backup withholding is required on winnings from slot machines, keno, and bingo, even though winnings from these games are not subject to regular withholding. Such withholding is required if you have net winnings of at least $1,200 from bingo or slot machines or $1,500 from keno.

Backup withholding is also required if you win more than $5,000 from a poker tournament and fail to furnish your ID to the sponsor.

Backup withholding applies to your winnings reduced by the amount wagered if the casino or other gambling establishment chooses to make that reduction.

*EXAMPLE: Barry wins $1,200 on a single spin at a slot machine in the Lady Luck Casino. Casino personnel inform him that a Form W-2G must be filed with the IRS and ask him for his Social Security number. He refuses to tell them his number. As a result, the casino must withhold 28% from his winnings and pay it to the IRS. The amount withheld is $336 ($1,200 X 28%). If Barry furnished his Social Security number, no withholding would be required.*

##  Do you have to show your Social Security card?

It's usually not a good idea to carry your Social Security card around with you since, if you lose it, someone might use it to commit identity theft. The IRS does not require that you show your original Social Security card to casino personnel when they complete Form W-2G. It's sufficient for you tell them or write down the number. You need not have any written proof of the number.

Unfortunately, some casino personnel—especially at Indian casinos—don't understand this and require you to show your actual Social Security card to avoid backup withholding. If this happens, ask to speak to supervisor and explain the situation. If a casino refuses to accept your word about your number, you can ask to fill out IRS Form W-9, *Request for Taxpayer Identification Number*. You list your Social Security number and sign this form. By signing, you certify under penalty for perjury that you have provided the correct number. You can download and print out blank copies of the W-9 from the IRS website at www.irs.gov.

| IRS Income Tax Withholding Rules for Gambling | | |
|---|---|---|
| **Type of Game** | **Regular 28% (25% in 2010 and earlier) withholding required if winnings are:** | **Backup withholding at 28% if winner does not provide tax ID number and winnings are:** |
| Slot machines | N/A | ≥$1,200 |
| Keno | N/A | ≥$1,500 |
| Bingo | N/A | ≥$1,200 |
| Sweepstakes, wagering pools, lotteries, raffles | | $600 to $5,000 |
| Poker tournaments | N/A if winnings reported on form W-2G | >$5,000 |
| All other wagers when winnings are at least 300 times the amount bet | >$5,000 | $600 to $5,000 |

Some states have withholding, too

Several states automatically withhold state income tax from gambling winnings whenever a Form W-2G is filed. This is so whether or not the winner is a state resident. See Chapter 7 for details.

# Determining Your Annual Wins and Losses

When you do your taxes you are supposed to list your total annual gambling wins and losses on your return (if you itemize your deductions). Your total wins and losses for the year must be tracked separately and kept separate on your return. This leads to a seemingly simple question: How do you figure out how much you won and lost during the year? Unfortunately, the answer to this question is not so simple.

Read this chapter carefully. Although this information may seem boring and technical, how you track your wins and losses will determine whether you owe the IRS any taxes on your winnings. Doing it wrong could cost you dearly.

## Wins and Losses Are Tracked by the Session

Here's the basic rule: You figure out how much you've won and lost gambling during the entire year by keeping track of all your wins and losses for each gambling session you have. You add up all your winning sessions during the year to determine your total annual winnings. You add together all your losing sessions during the year to determine your annual losses. You don't consider any sessions in which you broke even. Wins and losses are always kept separate. Do not subtract one from the other.

It makes no difference what type of gambling you do—slot machines, blackjack, online poker, bingo, or the lottery. A gambling session is a gambling session—all the IRS cares about is whether you won or lost (or broke even).

For example, if you had 10 gambling sessions during the year in which you won a total of $10,000, you have $10,000 in total gambling winnings for the year. If you had another 10 sessions in which you lost a total of $9,000, you have annual losses of $9,000. These are the numbers the IRS wants to see on your tax return, not your actual net gambling winnings for the year of $1,000. However, you can deduct your loses up to the amount of your winnings, and thereby offset your winnings for tax purposes—provided you have enough losses (see Chapter 6).

# What Is a Gambling Session?

Obviously, it's vitally important to understand what constitutes a gambling session for tax purposes. Unfortunately, neither the IRS nor courts have ever provided definitive guidance on this issue. On one hand, you are not required to keep track of every bet you make (which would probably be impossible). On the other hand, you may not total your winnings and losses by the gambling trip, or by the week, month, or year.

Gamblers have to use their common sense and what guidance the IRS and courts have provided to arrive at a definition of a gambling session that the IRS is likely to accept. It may not be the same definition that every gambler uses, but as long as it is reasonable and you use it consistently, it will probably satisfy the IRS.

### Basic rule

Based on recent IRS guidance and court rulings, here's a common-sense definition of a gambling session that is likely acceptable: *For a recreational gambler, a gambling session lasts for any period of continuous play without cashing out. However, a session cannot last more than one day.*

For example, let's say you enter a casino with $100 in your pocket and play the slot machines for one hour. You end up dumping your entire $100 into the machines. When you cash in your tickets, you have a total of $300. You had one gambling session in which you won $200. This is true even though you may have had $1,000 in winning spins and $700 in losing spins during the course of play.

To determine how much you've won or lost when you cash out, you add together the amount of your original buy-in plus any additional money you bet, whether cash you brought with you or cash you added at the casino from markers, ATM draws, credit card advances, or cashing checks.

For example, you enter a casino with $100 in your pocket and play the slot machines for one hour. You lose the $100 in the first five minutes and make a $100 withdrawal from an ATM to continue playing. You leave the casino with $300. You've won $100 during your gambling session—$200 buy-ins minus $300 cash-out.

##  Legal Authority

If you're audited by the IRS and the auditor questions how you've defined a session, point out that there is legal authority for this definition. First, in IRS Chief Counsel Memorandum 2008-11, the IRS's own legal office concluded that "a casual gambler playing a slot machine... recognizes a wagering gain or loss at the time she redeems her tokens." This memorandum is not a legal precedent and may not be relied upon in court, but it does show the IRS's current position on this issue. Moreover, the Chief Counsel's reasoning was accepted by the Tax Court in Shollenberger v. Comm'r, TC Memo 2009-306.

Applying this rule, a gambling session can last for as little as a few seconds or as much as several days. It depends on how long you play continuously without cashing out. Moreover, if you play several different games or in several different casinos during the course of a day and cash out multiple times, you'll have multiple sessions for that day.

Example: Jane enters the Tropicana Casino in Las Vegas on September 1. Over the next five hours she plays blackjack, video poker, craps, slot machines, and roulette, cashing out after she finishes playing each game. She switches blackjack dealers several times and plays at six different slot machines. She need not count her play at each table or machine as a session. Rather, she counts all the time she continuously played the same game without cashing out as a session. Calculated this way, she had five sessions for the day. As the chart below shows, she had two winning sessions of $900 and $1,500, and three losing sessions of $1,000, $595, and $700. All her winning and losing sessions must be kept track of separately, with the annual totals separately reported on her tax return. The fact that she ended up with net winnings of $5 for the day is meaningless for tax purposes.

| Date | Game | Buy-In | Cash-Out | Won | Lost |
|------|------|--------|----------|-----|------|
| 9/1 | Blackjack | $100 | $1,000 | $900 | |
| 9/1 | Video Poker | $1,400 | $300 | | $1,100 |
| 9/1 | Craps | $10 | $1,510 | $1,500 | |
| 9/1 | Slot Machines | $600 | $5 | | $595 |
| 9/1 | Roulette | $2,000 | $1,300 | | $700 |
| 9/1 | **TOTAL** | | | $2,400 | $2,395 |

Why Long Gambling Sessions Are Better Than Short Ones

The more gambling sessions you have, the more winnings and losses you'll have for tax purposes. The winnings will increase your annual income for the year. If your total winnings are substantial, you could end up losing valuable tax deductions and credits because your income is too high. This can be true even if you were a net loser at gambling for the year! (See Chapter 6 for a detailed discussion.) The longer your sessions, the fewer there will be, and you'll likely have lower total wins and losses to report to the IRS.

Let's look at how to apply our rule to various types of games.

### Slot machines, video poker and other machine games

Machine games include slot machines and video poker. The IRS does not expect you to keep track of every pull you take at a slot machine or every video poker hand. You can treat as one session any time period of continuous slot machine play at the same location, no matter how many machines you play. However, a session can't last more than one day.

*EXAMPLE: Ralph goes to a casino and continuously plays the slots machines for three hours. During this time he played 12 different slot machines. He may treat his entire three hours of continuous play as one gambling session.*

## Table games

Table games include blackjack, craps, roulette, and baccarat. A table game session lasts as long as you play the same game and don't cash in your chips, even though you play at more than one table. So long as you play the same game, your gambling session can last many hours, even an entire day. But, the moment you stop playing, cash in your chips, or switch to another game, your session ends. Once the session ends, you subtract your total losses from your winnings to determine your winnings or losses for that session.

> *EXAMPLE: Samantha goes to a Las Vegas casino to play black-jack. She plays table 1 for 10 minutes and loses $100. She then switches to table 2 and wins $50 in 20 minutes. She then hops to table 3 and loses $90 over the next hour. She then leaves table 3 to play craps. She may treat her continuous blackjack play at all three tables as one gambling session. She had $190 in losses and $50 in winnings; thus, she has a $140 loss for the blackjack session.*

If you play in a blackjack tournament, use the rules for poker tournaments described below.

## Poker

Poker, of course, is not one game buy many, and it can be played in various formats. This makes the defining a gambling session for poker difficult.

**Live Games**: In a live or "ring" poker game, the players at a single table compete against themselves, and players can leave the game and cash in their chips at any time. For live games, a session lasts as long as you continuously play the same game and don't cash in your chips, no matter how many tables at which you play or how many times you change stakes.

*EXAMPLE: Jill goes to a card room at an Atlantic City casino and continuously plays Texas Hold'em at five different tables over four hours. She treats her entire period of continuous Texas Hold'em play as one gambling session. During the four hours her buy-ins totaled $1,000 and she had $500 in chips when she cashed in. Jill lost $500 for the session.*

**Tournament Play:** All the players in a poker tournament compete against each other, instead of against just the players at each table. Each player pays an entry fee to enter the tournament and is given a certain amount in chips to play with. However, the players can't cash in their chips. Instead, each player continues to play until he loses all his chips or wins the tournament. The player or players with the most chips at the end of the tournament receive specified prizes.

Treat an entire poker tournament as one gambling session, even though you'll probably change tables many times during the tournament. Your entry fee constitutes your buy-in. If you win a prize, you subtract the entry free from the value of your prize to determine you net winnings for the session. If you don't win a prize, your loss is equal to the amount of your entry fee. For example, if you pay $1,000 to enter a tournament and win a $5,000 prize, your winnings for the session are $4,000. If you win nothing, you have a $1,000 loss.

### Internet gambling

You can do almost any kind of gambling on the Internet, but poker is the most popular. For cash games, count all the time you play the same game in one continuous sitting as one session, no matter how many tables you play. Count play at different games (Omaha, Texas Hold'em, etc.) as different sessions. Online poker tournaments should be treated the same as any other tournaments—each tournament is one session.

### Horse races and dog races

If you bet on horse or dog races, the IRS considers each separate race to be a gambling session, as is each combination bet on multiple races. For example, if you spend all day at the track and bet on every race (nine in all), you'll have nine separate gambling sessions.

*EXAMPLE: Johnny goes to his local race track and bets on three races. He wins $50 on the first race, loses $100 on the second race, and wins $50 on the third race. He broke even for the day. But, since each race is a gambling session, for tax purposes he had $100 of winnings and $100 in losses. These amounts should be included with all his other gambling winnings and losses for the year.*

If you make more than one bet on a single race, you subtract the cost of all the tickets you purchased from the amount you won (if any) to determine your total win or loss for that race.

Combination bets covering two or more races, such as daily doubles and pick-six, each constitute a gambling session.

## Sports betting

Treat sports betting the same as horse or dog race betting. Each game or other sporting event should be treated as a separate session.

*EXAMPLE: Sid loves to bet on the NFL. One week he bet on three different games. Each game constitutes a single gambling session. He won $100 on the first game, lost $25 on the second, and lost $75 on the third game. For tax purposes, he had three gambling sessions. He has winnings of $100 and losses of $100 for the day.*

If you make multiple bets on the same game, subtract the amount of all the bets you made from the amount you won (if any) to determine your total win or loss for that game.

## Bingo

To play bingo, you have to purchase one or more bingo cards, also called tickets. These can be purchased individually or in packs or books containing many cards that can be used for multiple bingo games. The cost of these cards is the amount of your wager or "buy-in." Thus, if you win a bingo game, your net winnings are equal to your total winnings less the cost of the card(s).

Many individual bingo games are ordinarily played in the course of an hour or an evening in a bingo hall or other gaming establishment. Treat all the games played with that pack as a single gambling session. If you buy multiple bingo packs you can treat them like a single pack if you play them all at the same time. If the total amount you've won in all the games played with the pack exceeds the cost of the pack, you have a net win for the session. If you have no winnings or they are less than the cost of the pack, you have a loss.

Instant bingo games, also called pull-tabs, or scratchers are more like lotteries than traditional bingo. The rules for lotteries discussed below apply.

### Lotteries

Treat each lottery drawing as a single gambling session, no matter how many tickets you purchase.

*EXAMPLE: Vicki spends $90 for 30 tickets for a state lottery drawing held on July 1. She wins $500. Her total win for tax purposes is $410.*

### Keno

Use the same rules for as for horse racing or bingo.

## Gambling Sessions Do Not Track W-2Gs

The casino or other gambling establishment will issue you a IRS Form W-2G if you win more than a specified amount on a *single bet*—for example, you'll receive a W-2G if you win $1,200 or more on a single slot machine spin. This has nothing to do with a gambling session, which can be one bet or hundreds depending on how long you play continuously. It's not uncommon for a gambler to be issued a Form W-2G during a session and end up losing all the money listed on the form by the time the session ends.

> *EXAMPLE: Jack enters the Lady Luck Casino at 10:00 a.m. with $100 in his pocket and starts playing the slot machines. At 11:00 he wins a $1,500 jackpot and is issued a Form W-2G by the casino. He continues playing until 1:00. He cashes in his tickets and leaves the casino with $5 in his pocket. Thus, he ended up losing the entire $1,500 jackpot plus $95 of his original $100 stake. He had one gambling session in which he lost $95.*

Although Form W-2Gs are not issued by the session, and the money reported can be lost before a session ends, the numbers on the forms are still reported to the IRS and inputted into its computers. This can cause problems if the total for all your winning sessions during the year is less than the amount on the W-2Gs sent to the IRS. How to deal with this is covered in Chapter 6.

# Documenting Your Wins and Losses

This chapter explains why and how to document your gambling wins and losses. Ideally, this involves two elements: (1) keeping a gambling log, and (2) obtaining and saving back-up documentation for the log.

## Why Bother?

It's likely that less than one recreational gambler in 100 keeps all the documentation described in this chapter. It takes time and trouble and is no fun. So why bother? Here's why: It's up to you to prove to the IRS how much you lost gambling during the year. The casinos where you play won't do it for you, although their records can be helpful. If you don't provide adequate proof of your claimed losses, the IRS will likely disallow them and force you to pay taxes on all your reported winnings—tax you wouldn't have to pay if you had kept good records.

By far, the number one reason gamblers have trouble with the IRS is because they don't have adequate records of their wins and losses. Here's a common scenario: Jack is a recreational gambler who never keeps any records of his play. During a visit to the Lady Luck Casino he gets lucky and wins $5,000 on a single play at video poker. The casino files a Form W-2G reporting his win to the IRS. Six months later, Jack does his taxes. He's sure he lost more than he won during the year, so he lists $5,000 of gambling winnings on his return and $5,000 in losses. He gets audited and the IRS asks him for proof he lost at least $5,000 gambling. He has none, so the IRS disallows his clamed losses. As a result, he must pay income tax on his $5,000 in winnings.

Of course, if you never win enough to have a Form W-2G filed with the IRS by the casino or other gambling establishment, the IRS will likely never question you about your gambling winnings and losses. It probably won't know that you gambled at all. If you've never been issued a Form W-2G you may be thinking that it's not worth the trouble to keep gambling records. But here's the problem: You never know when you'll win big and end up with a Form W-2G. This can happen at any time. For example, if you're a slot player it will happen any time you win $1,200 on a single play. You say this has never happened to you? So what. It can happen the next time you go to the casino.

You should view gambling documentation as a form of insurance; but in this instance it's insurance that protects you if something good happens—you have a big win. The bigger your win, the more you'll wish you had good documentation of your losses.

## Keeping a Gambling Log or Diary

Starting right now you should keep a log or diary recording how much you win or lose during each gambling session. This will not only help you if you're audited by IRS, it will also (1) help you when you do your taxes for the year, (2) enable you to know exactly how much you are winning and losing, and (3) provide data you can use to analyze your play and become a better gambler.

Your log should be created contemporaneously with your gambling—that is, during or soon after each gambling session. You can't wait until the end of the year, or when you're audited, to create one from memory and whatever records you have.

If you and your spouse both gamble, you should each keep a separate log. When you do your taxes, you'll be able to combine your winnings and losses on your joint tax return.

The log should not be filed with your tax return. Just keep it in a safe place so you'll have it to show the IRS if it questions your gambling income or losses.

Internet gambling records

If you gamble on the internet, you may be in luck. Many online casinos provide online logs to their players that enable them to keep track of all their transactions and play. Print these out periodically—every week or month—and keep them with your other gambling records. Also, you may be able to take screen shots while you're logged into your online casino. These can serve as additional supporting documentation.

### Log formats

There is no single format the IRS requires for a gambling log. Your log can be handwritten in a notebook, appointment book, calendar, or any other piece of paper in which you write down how much you won or lost for each gambling session. You can also purchase gambling log books.

If you use a handwritten log, write it in pen, not pencil. There shouldn't be erasures—if you make a mistake cross it out. The pages in your log should be sequentially numbered and no pages should be torn out.

The IRS prefers handwritten logs because they are difficult to create after the fact if you get audited. However, you can use a computerized log—for example, you can create a spreadsheet to record your wins and losses. There is also specialized software for recording poker winnings and losses such as PokerTracker (see www. pokertracker.com). You can also combine paper and electronic records—for example, you can make notes of your wins and losses in a diary or calendar, and then list them all on a computer spreadsheet.

### Log contents

For each gambling session, the IRS says you should record in your log the:

- date
- name and address (or location) of the gambling establishment
- type of wager(s) you made
- amount(s) you won or lost during each gambling session, and
- names of any other people with you during the session. (Rev. Proc. 77-29.)

Remember, you record your wins or losses *by the gambling session.* What constitutes a gambling session depends on what game you play and how long you play. If you don't understand what a gambling session is, review Chapter 4.

The information listed above is the minimum the IRS wants you to record. But, it would like even more if you play slots or table games. If you play slot machines, the IRS says you should note the machine number and time you started and ended your play. For table games such as blackjack, craps, roulette and Wheel of Fortune, the IRS wants you to make a note of the table number. Few people other than professional gamblers actually do this; but if you do you'll go to the head of the IRS class.

## Keep Records for Home Games

If you play poker for money at home or engage in illegal sports betting, you should keep careful track of your wins and losses. Your losses from illegal gambling are just as deductible as those from a casino. Likewise, your wins are taxable. The IRS won't report you to the police if it learns you engage in illegal gambling. All it wants is its cut of your winnings.

Here's an example of a log format you can use for most types of casino gambling, including slots:

| Date | Time | Location | Game | Net Win | Net Loss | W-2Gs | Accompanied by |
|------|------|----------|------|---------|----------|-------|----------------|
|      |      |          |      |         |          |       |                |
|      |      |          |      |         |          |       |                |

*EXAMPLE: Jack spends a long weekend in Las Vegas where he meets up with a couple of lady friends. Over three days he plays slots, craps, blackjack, Keno, video poker, and makes a sports bet. He keeps track of the games he plays and his wins and losses on a small pocket calendar he carries with him. At the end of his trip, he transfers the information to a computer spreadsheet.*

| | A | B | C | D | E | F | G | H |
|---|---|---|---|---|---|---|---|---|
| 1 | Date | Time | Location | Game | Net Win | Net Loss | W-2Gs | Accompanied by |
| 2 | 2/1/11 | 9:00-10:30 p.m. | Lady Luck Casino, LV | Slots | 1,050 | | 1,200 | Eve Arden |
| 3 | | 10:30-11:00 | Pair-a-Dice Casino, LV | Craps | | 100 | | Eve Arden |
| 4 | | 11:00-12:00 | | Blackjack | 200 | | | |
| 5 | 2/2/11 | 11:00-2:00 p.m. | Lady Luck Casino, LV | Slots | 1,950 | | 1,200 | Jane Doe |
| 6 | | 2:30 p.m. | | Keno | | 5 | | Jane Doe |
| 7 | | 3:00-3:30 | Pair-a-Dice Casino, LV | Video Poker | | 200 | | |
| 8 | | 3:30-5:30 | | Slots | | 1,000 | | Kim Philby |
| 9 | | | | Cashback | | | 100 | |
| 10 | 2/3/11 | 5:00 p.m. | Airport Sports Book, LV | Sports Bet | | 1,000 | | |

Here is a format for a log you can use for horse and dog racing. Each race and combination bet is considered a separate session.

| Date | Location | Game | Race Number | Amount Wagered | Net Win | Net Loss | W-2Gs |
|---|---|---|---|---|---|---|---|
| 2/1/2011 | Santa Anita | Horse Racing | 1 | $50 | $1,050 | | |
| 2/1/2011 | Santa Anita | Horses | Pick Six | $50 | | $50 | |

## Back-Up Documentation for Your Gambling Log

Many people believe that all they have to do to prove their gambling wins and losses is keep an accurate gambling log. This is not the case. Because you create your gambling log yourself, it may not be accurate. After all, you have a strong incentive to minimize your winnings and maximize your losses so you can avoid paying taxes. The IRS is well aware of this, so it wants you to back up the information in your log with documentation you didn't create yourself. In the event of an audit, it will double check this documentation against what you've recorded in your log to help verify whether the log is truthful. Your back-up documentation need not—and likely will not—verify every entry in your log; but it should help convince the IRS that you haven't made up everything in your log. Don't file this documentation with your tax return. Just keep it handy in case the IRS questions your gambling wins and losses.

You don't necessarily have to keep all the documentation described below—few gamblers do. However, the more you have the better off you'll be if you get audited. Here is the back-up documentation the IRS would like you to keep:

- Evidence that shows that you really were at the casino or other gambling establishment at which you claim you gambled—for example, airplane tickets to your gambling destination, dated parking receipts when you parked at a casino or other gambling establishment, copies of your hotel reservations and billing statements, dinner and snack shop receipts, and any other information that will show you were at the casino that day.

- Copies of all IRS Form W-2G, *Certain Gambling Winnings*, casinos or other gaming establishments gave you when you won more than a threshold amount (see Chapter 2)
- Copies of IRS Form 5754, *Statement by Person(s) Receiving Gambling Winnings*, that is used when you win more than a threshold amount on a group wager (see Chapter 2)
- wagering tickets
- canceled checks you wrote to pay for wagers
- credit records showing advances of credit to you from casinos or other gaming establishments
- bank withdrawal records (including ATM receipts), and
- statements of actual winnings or payment slips provided to you by gambling establishments.

The IRS would also like you to keep the following documentation for particular games:

- *Keno*: Keep copies of keno tickets you purchased that were validated by the gambling establishment, copies of your casino credit records, and copies of your casino check cashing records.
- *Table games (twenty-one, blackjack, craps, poker, baccarat, roulette, wheel of fortune, etc.):* If you gambled on credit, keep casino credit card data indicating whether the credit was issued in the pit or at the cashier's cage (this will ordinarily apply only if you're a "high roller").
- *Poker tournaments:* Ask for and keep receipts for all your buy-ins to enter poker tournaments.
- *Bingo:* Keep all your receipts from the casino or bingo parlor.

- *Racing (horse, harness, dog, etc.):* Keep your unredeemed tickets and payment records from the racetrack. Make a habit of stapling to the day's official track program all of your losing tickets, winning receipts, and any other documentation you obtain. Be sure to save the programs.
- *Lotteries:* Keep unredeemed tickets, payment slips, and winnings statements. Don't throw away your losing tickets, including instant scratch-off tickets, daily game tickets, and Big Game and Lotto tickets. Put them all in a manila envelope and save them.

##  Use a checking account for gambling

A great way to keep track of exactly how much you spend on gambling during the year is to open a separate checking account just for gambling. When you need money to gamble with, write a check to this account. Don't use money from any other source. Your statements will provide you with a record of how much you spent on gambling during the year.

# Casino Win-Loss Statements

If you're like most gamblers today, you use a rewards card (also called a player's card or slot club card) during all or most of your play at casinos. If you don't, you should start. Most gamblers use a rewards card because it can help them get comps. However, using a rewards card can also enable you to get a record of your play from the casino.

If you so request, after the end of the year the casino will send you an annual win-loss statement. Such a statement is an estimate of what you won or lost at the casino during the year based on the casino's player tracking information. The casino gathers this information when you use your rewards card to play slots and other machine games, or ask casino personnel to manually keep track of your play when you play table games, keno, or sports betting. You can usually obtain the statement by filling out a form on the casino's website or calling or writing the casino. Here is an example of a win-loss statement issued by Harrah's Casino.

| GAMING HISTORY STATEMENT FOR THE YEAR 2002 | | | | | |
|---|---|---|---|---|---|
| WIN OR LOSS TOTAL ($45,655.40) | TOTAL REWARDS NUMBER XXXXXXXXX | | | | W2G TOTAL $4,216.00 |
| LOCATION | NET SLOT WIN or (LOSS) | NET GAMES WIN or (LOSS) | NET OTHER WIN or (LOSS) | TOTAL WIN or (LOSS) | TOTAL W2G |
| BLUFFS RUN CASINO, IA | ($241.00) | $0.00 | $0.00 | ($241.00) | $0.00 |
| HARRAH'S, ATLANTIC CITY, NJ | ($2,578.75) | $0.00 | $0.00 | ($2,578.75) | $0.00 |
| HARRAH'S, CHEROKEE, NC | ($178.00) | $0.00 | $0.00 | ($178.00) | $0.00 |
| HARRAH'S, COUNCIL BLUFFS, IA | ($1,228.00) | $0.00 | $0.00 | ($1,228.00) | $0.00 |
| HARRAH'S, EAST CHICAGO, IN | ($9,949.00) | $0.00 | $0.00 | ($9,949.00) | $0.00 |
| HARRAH'S, JOLIET, IL | ($3,102.00) | $0.00 | $0.00 | ($3,102.00) | $0.00 |
| HARRAH'S, LAKE CHARLES, LA | ($2,122.00) | $0.00 | $0.00 | ($2,122.00) | $0.00 |
| HARRAH'S, LAKE TAHOE, NV | ($3,267.00) | $0.00 | $0.00 | ($3,267.00) | $0.00 |
| HARRAH'S, LAS VEGAS, NV | ($9,653.00) | $0.00 | $0.00 | ($9,653.00) | $4,216.00 |
| HARRAH'S, LAUGHLIN, NV | ($6,804.00) | $0.00 | $0.00 | ($6,804.00) | $0.00 |
| HARRAH'S, METROPOLIS, IL | ($522.00) | $0.00 | $0.00 | ($522.00) | $0.00 |
| HARRAH'S, NEW ORLEANS, LA | ($1,384.00) | $0.00 | $0.00 | ($1,384.00) | $0.00 |
| HARRAH'S, NORTH KANSAS CITY, MO | ($2,480.00) | $0.00 | $0.00 | ($2,480.00) | $0.00 |
| HARRAH'S, PRAIRIE-TOPEKA, KS | ($466.00) | $0.00 | $0.00 | ($466.00) | $0.00 |
| HARRAH'S, RENO, NV | ($72.00) | $0.00 | $0.00 | ($72.00) | $0.00 |
| HARRAH'S, RINCON-SAN DIEGO, CA | ($53.00) | $0.00 | $0.00 | ($53.00) | $0.00 |
| HARRAH'S, SHREVEPORT, LA | ($995.00) | $0.00 | $0.00 | ($995.00) | $0.00 |
| HARRAH'S, ST. LOUIS, MO | $168.00 | $0.00 | $0.00 | $168.00 | $0.00 |
| HARRAH'S, VICKSBURG, MS | ($324.00) | $0.00 | $0.00 | ($324.00) | $0.00 |
| HARVEYS, LAKE TAHOE, NV | ($57.00) | $0.00 | $0.00 | ($57.00) | $0.00 |
| RIO, LAS VEGAS, NV | ($639.00) | $0.00 | $0.00 | ($639.00) | $0.00 |
| SHOWBOAT, ATLANTIC CITY, NJ | $321.35 | $0.00 | $0.00 | $321.35 | $0.00 |
| | | | | ($45,655.40) | $4,216.00 |

Most recreational gamblers don't keep good records on their own. Thus, casino win-loss statements are often the only records they have of their gambling wins and losses. Although win-loss statements are better than nothing and can help corroborate your gambling log, they do not take the place of a gambling log. Casino win-loss statements are not as good as a gambling log because:

- the IRS doesn't have to accept them
- they usually are not accurate
- they inflate your winnings, and
- they contain disclaimers.

##  What is a rewards card?

Today, all casinos, and many other gambling establishments such as race-tracks, are highly computerized. Virtually all casinos have slot clubs. Players sign up and receive a free rewards card, which they insert into special electronic readers on each slot and video poker machine they play. The card identifies the player and the casino automatically keeps a computerized record of wins and losses when the card is in the machine.

In most casinos, you can also use your rewards card to track your play at table games, keno or sports betting by asking the pit boss to rate your play at these games. The pit boss will observe your average bet during one or two hands or plays and input this information into the casino computers. The computer will use this number to extrapolate how much you bet during your gambling session.

By using their rewards card, gamblers accumulate points that can be redeemed for cash, gifts, free rooms, free food, and other comps.

## The IRS doesn't have to accept win-loss statements

The trend today is for the IRS and courts to accept casino win-loss statements and use them to help calculate a taxpayer's gambling wins and losses during the year. In one case, for example, an IRS auditor denied all of a couple's claimed gambling losses for 2005 and 2006 because they did not keep a gambling log. They didn't have a log for 2007 either, but they used a player's card to gamble that year and were able to provide casino win-loss statements for their play that year. The auditor accepted the figures on these statements and allowed the reported losses. (*Bain v. Comm'r,* TCM 091299D (June 10, 2010).)

However, neither the IRS nor courts have to accept win-loss statement as evidence of your wins and losses, and in many cases they have refused to do so. In one case, for example, the Tax Court refused to accept at face value a win-loss statement a gambler provided from the Foxwoods Casino stating that the she had lost $35,480 at slots during one year. Noting that the statement failed to list the gambler's wins or losses for each gambling session as required by the IRS, the court said that "[n]o valid reason exists for taxpayers engaged in wagering transactions not to maintain a contemporaneous gambling diary or gambling log." (*LaPlante v. Comm'r,* TCM 2009-226.)

## Win-Loss statements are inaccurate

Casino win-loss statements are notoriously inaccurate. Many gamblers who keep detailed records of their wins and losses find that the statements bear little relationship to reality. No one knows this better than the casinos themselves. Here's what the MGM Mirage Casino says about its statements:

> *"Your statement reflects only gaming recorded when a Players Club card was either inserted correctly into the slot machine or a manual rating was created in the table games area of the casino. This does not include slot tournament winnings, giveaway party winnings, race and sports book activity, poker activity, or keno activity. Therefore, this statement does not reflect an accurate accounting record. It merely provides an estimate that you can use to compare to your own records."*

Because you don't have to use a rewards card to play, there is no way for the IRS to know whether a win-loss statement you submit records all, or only some, of your play. Moreover, a rewards card can be used by anyone.

## Win-Loss statements inflate your winnings

The winnings shown on casino win-loss statements can be larger than your true winnings, which can cost you more taxes. This is because of the way your wins and losses are calculated by the casino. Win-loss statements are not calculated by the gambling session, as required by the IRS. Here's how the Bellagio calculates the annual totals on its win-loss statements: *"The formula to determine your net slot win-loss is calculated by taking total coin paid out of the ma-*

*chines, plus jackpots paid by hand currency, less total coin deposited into the machines (this total may include any and all jackpots)."*

In other words, the casino adds all the money you put in the machines during the year ("coin in") and subtracts from it all the money you took out ("coin out"). Coin-in is not only the out-of-pocket money you play through the machine, but also anything you win and re-play through the machine. This method of tracking your wins and losses results in the same coin being counted multiple times which will overstate the amount of your wins and losses.

### Win-Loss statements contain disclaimers

Because they are frequently inaccurate, casinos refuse to stand behind their win-loss statements. They come with disclaimers stating that the casino does not guarantee their accuracy or that the IRS will accept them as proof of your losses. Here is a disclaimer used by Harrah's:

*"DISCLAIMER: The estimated win-loss is based upon information provided by Harrah's player tracking system. This does not include any activity when Harrah's Total Rewards card is not inserted properly in the card reader. This amount may not include all hand paid jackpots reportable to the Internal Revenue Service on form W2G. This player tracking system is a marketing tool and, therefore, we make no representation as to either the accuracy of this information or its effectiveness as a report of losses. The IRS recommends keeping a diary of your gaming activity with such pertinent information as dates, slot machine or table numbers, jackpots, and total wins and losses."*

# Completing Your Tax Return

This chapter is where the rubber hits the road: it shows you how to report your gambling wins and losses on your tax return and figure out whether you need to pay income tax on your winnings. Because of the unfair and punitive way the tax law treats gamblers, you can end up owing more in taxes even if you were a net loser for the year from gambling. So, whether you prepare your return yourself or hire a tax pro to do your taxes, you need to understand this stuff.

This chapter is for casual gamblers. If you're professional gambler, turn to Chapter 8 for guidance on how to do your taxes.

Completing your tax return for gambling income and losses is a four step process:

- gathering your gambling documentation
- figuring your total annual gambling wins and losses
- deciding whether to itemize, and
- filling out your tax forms.

## Step 1: Gather Gambling Documentation

The first thing you need to do is gather together all your documentation of your gambling wins and losses during the past year.

If, throughout the year, you've kept the gambling log and back-up documentation suggested in Chapter 5, this step will be a snap. Just gather together your logs and documents along with your other tax documents.

However, if, like most casual gamblers, you have not kept good records, you'll have some work to do. If you do not have a gambling log, you need to gather as much of the documentation described below as soon as possible.

###  Do You Need More Time?

If you haven't kept good records and it's already near April 15, you may wish to obtain an automatic extension to file your taxes until October 15. This will give you six more months to get your records together. To obtain an extension, you simply file IRS Form 4868, *Application For Automatic Extension of Time To File U.S. Individual Tax Return.* You can file the form electronically or by postal mail. Whatever method you use, you must file your extension by April 15. You can download the form from the IRS website at http://www.irs.gov/pub/irs-pdf/f4868.pdf.

However, be aware an extension of time to file is not an extension of time to pay. You will owe interest on any past due tax and you may be subject to a late-payment penalty if you haven't paid all the taxes you owe by April 15. You may need to send in an extra payment along with your extension.

### Win-Loss statements

If, like most gamblers today, you use a rewards card when you gamble at casinos and other gambling establishments, you can obtain annual win-loss statements from the casinos you visited. As explained in Chapter 5, win-loss statements are not as good as a gambling log you prepare yourself, and can be inaccurate. Moreover, the IRS is not required to accept them. Nevertheless, they usually are accepted by the IRS. Also, they may be the only gambling records you can get.

You need to ask casinos and other gambling establishments to send you win-loss statements. They will not provide them automatically. Make a list of all the casinos you need to contact. You may need to gather together all the rewards cards you used during the year to make an accurate list.

Often, you can request your win-loss statement through the casino's website, or you may have to call the casino, or mail in a request. Check each casino's website to find out what procedure it uses.

You should make these requests as early in the year as possible, since it may take some casinos time to get their statements to you. Casinos are often inundated with requests near the April 15 tax filing deadline, so try not to wait until the last minute. If you get in all your requests by January 15, you should be able to get them all by February 28. If a casino doesn't send you your statement within a reasonable time, call them to find out what the problem is.

### W-2G Forms

Did you win enough the past year for any casinos or other gambling establishments to issue you any IRS forms W-2G or 1099-MISC? If so, make sure you have copies of all of these forms. You can be sure that the IRS has them. Ordinarily, the casino will give you your copies of the Form W-2G when you collect your jackpot. Most casinos will not mail you a separate Form W-2G. If you've lost one or more W-2G forms, you can contact the casino and ask for an additional copy. Check their website for contact details. If you aren't sure whether a particular casino issued you a W-2G, check your win-loss statement from the casino. It will usually show whether any Form W-2G have been filed.

### Other documentation

Even if you have kept an accurate gambling log, you need to have documentation to back it up. If you don't have a log, such documentation is even more important. This includes your bank statements, credit card records, canceled checks you wrote to pay for wagers, wagering tickets, credit records showing advances of credit to you from a casino or other gaming establishment, bank withdrawal records (including ATM receipts), and statements of actual winnings or payment slips provided to you by the gambling establishment. See Chapter 5 for a more detailed list of the back-up documentation that will help you in the event of an IRS audit.

## Step 2: Figure Your Total Wins and Losses

The most fundamental rule of tax reporting for gambling income is that all your wins and losses must be calculated separately and reported in separate places on your tax return. *You may not subtract your losses from your wins and list that number on your tax return.* This may seem counter-intuitive, but it's the rule. So, always, always keep your wins and losses separate.

First, add together the total amount of all your winning gambling sessions during the year. It makes no difference what type of gambling was involved or where you did it—in the U.S., a foreign country, or on the Internet. All gambling income, from whatever source, must be added together and reported on your tax return. You should also add to your winnings the total fair market value of any comps you received. Note that your total wins will not necessarily be the same as the total of any Form W-2Gs filed with the IRS by the casinos you visited (see below).

Next, add together all your losses—that is, add up all your losing gambling sessions. Don't include in your losses the expenses you incurred while you gambled—for example, the cost of travel or dealer tokes (tips). These expenses are not deductible by casual gamblers; the IRS says that they are nondeductible personal outlays.

If you and your spouse both gamble and you file a joint return, you should each figure your annual wins and losses separately. You then combine your wins and losses on your joint tax return.

If you kept careful track of all your gambling wins and loses session-by-session with a gambling log—as you should—it will be easy to figure your total wins and loses. Simply add together all your winning sessions recorded in your log, and add together all your losing sessions you've recorded.

If you don't have an accurate gambling log, try to come up with a reasonable estimate of your total annual wins and losses using casino win-loss statements and the other documentation described above—for example, your credit card and debit card statements, and Forms W-2G you were issued. (Note, however, that the amount of your Forms W-2G usually won't be the same as the amount of your actual winnings; see the sidebar below). How difficult it will be to come up with reasonable numbers depends on how much documentation you have. You may wish to have a tax pro help you with this.

At the end of this process you'll have two numbers: your annual gambling income (total winning sessions) and gambling losses (total losing sessions).

*EXAMPLE: Phil took 10 weekend trips to Las Vegas last year. He kept an accurate gambling log which shows that he had 10 winning gambling sessions and 20 losing sessions. He adds together all his winning sessions and determines that he won was $5,000. He adds all his losing sessions and ends up with total gambling losses of $10,000. These are the two numbers he needs for his tax return.*

##  Should You Just Use the Amount of Your Form W-2Gs?

A great many gamblers who don't keep good records report as their total gambling winnings only the total amount shown in the Form W-2Gs they received, even though they had other winnings as well. If they didn't get any W-2Gs, they report no gambling winnings at all. Many people who do this get away with it. But, obviously, it is not what you're supposed to do. The IRS knows that it's virtually certain that you had winnings other than the amounts reported on your Form W-2Gs. If you're audited, the fact that you only reported your W-2G winnings will make you look suspect to the IRS and courts and likely result in harsher treatment than if you had honestly reported all your winnings.

# Step 3: Decide Whether to Itemize

There's a sad truth about gambling taxation that most people don't understand: Your losses are not always deductible. You can deduct your gambling losses only if you itemize your deductions on your tax return. If you don't itemize, you can't deduct them, but you're still required to report and pay taxes on your winnings. If this sound grossly unfair, that's because it is.

### Standard deduction vs. itemizing

First, a little background. Everybody gets to deduct a certain amount from their taxes each year to account for various personal expenses. There are two different ways to get this deduction. First, you can itemize your personal deductions. To do this, you add up all your deductible personal expenses, list them on IRS Schedule A, and deduct them from your taxable income. Common deductible expenses include home mortgage interest, property taxes, medical expenses, and charitable contributions.

However, instead of keeping track of all such expenses, you are allowed to take the standard deduction: this is a specified amount taxpayers may deduct each year—a process called "itemizing." If you take the standard deduction, you don't have to file Schedule A, which makes your tax return much simpler.

When you file your taxes, it's up to you to decide whether to take the standard deduction or itemize your personal deductions. You can itemize in some years and take the standard deduction in others. The IRS doesn't care which option you choose. Obviously, you should choose the method that gives you the largest deduction.

## How much is the standard deduction?

The amount of your standard deduction depends on your filing status. The amount is also adjusted for inflation each year. The following chart shows the standard deduction amounts for 2010 and 2011.

| Filing Status | Standard Deduction 2010 | Standard Deduction 2011 |
|---|---|---|
| Single | $5,700 | $5,800 |
| Married filing jointly | $11,400 | $11,600 |
| Head of Household | $8,400 | $8,500 |
| Married filing separately | $5,700 | $5,800 |

If you're single or a head of household and are 65 or older, you get to increase your standard deduction by $1,450. If you're blind, you get an additional $1,450 increase. If you're married, a widow, or widower you get to increase your standard deduction by $1,150 for each spouse who is 65 or older, and by an additional $1,150 for each spouse who is blind.

## When to itemize

So, when should you itemize? Only when your total itemized deductions, including deductible gambling losses, exceed your allowable standard deduction. If your total itemized deductions are less than the standard deduction, don't itemize. This means you can't deduct your gambling losses. But you'll still come out ahead because you'll get a larger total tax deduction from the standard deduction.

Thus, for example, if you're a single taxpayer with a $5,700 standard deduction, you should itemize only if all your itemized deductions, including your allowable gambling losses, exceed $5,700.

Some people—about 30% of all taxpayers—itemize every year. These are people with substantial itemized deductions such as home mortgage interest, property tax, medical expenses, and unreimbursed employee expenses. If you're in this category, then itemizing will be a no-brainer. Just add your deductible losses to your Schedule A.

However, the majority of taxpayers don't itemize because their total itemized deductions are less than the standard deduction. Indeed, lots of taxpayers have few or no itemized deductions at all. If you usually don't itemize your deductions you'll need to figure out whether to do so for any year you have gambling losses.

You'll need to determine the total amount you'd be allowed to deduct if you elect to itemize. First, determine your deductible gambling losses—these are the amount of your losses *up to your total winnings for the year.* You get no deduction for any losses that exceed your annual winnings. For example, if you lost $50,000 and won $10,000 last year, you only get to deduct $10,000 of your losses. The remaining $40,000 in losses is not deductible for this or any other year.

If your deductible losses exceed the standard deduction, then you should itemize. But, if they are less than the standard deduction, you'll need to add to your deductible losses the amount of any other itemized deductions you can take. If the total exceeds the standard deduction, you'll want to itemize. Otherwise, stick with the standard deduction.

Figuring out which other itemized deductions you can take may not be so easy because there are many different deductions and there are limits on how much you can deduct for many of them. The most common itemized deductions are home mortgage interest, property taxes, other state and local taxes, charitable donations, and unreimbursed medical expenses. There are also various miscellaneous itemized deductions, including some education expenses, unreimbursed employee expenses, union or professional dues, and investing expenses.

Some of these deductions are subject to special limitations. For example, medical expenses are deductible only to the extent they exceed 7.5% of your adjusted gross income. Miscellaneous itemized deductions are deductible only to the extent they exceed 2% of your AGI. Your gambling winnings are included in your AGI, so the more you win the harder it is to take these deductions (see below). Fortunately, gambling losses are not subject to any percentage of AGI limits. You may deduct all your gambling losses up to the amount of your winnings as an itemized deduction on Schedule A. For a more detailed discussion of itemized deductions, refer to IRS Publication 17, *Your Federal Income Tax*. You can download it from the IRS website at www.irs.gov.

You can use software such as TurboTax to calculate the total amount of your itemized deductions, or have a tax pro do it for you.

EXAMPLE 1: Bill, a single taxpayer, had 20 gambling sessions last year. He had five winning sessions in which he won a total of $1,000. He had 15 losing sessions in which he lost $5,000. His total deductible gambling losses are $1,000—his losses up to the amount of his total winnings. Bill has no itemized deductions other than his gambling losses. Thus, his total itemized deductions are only $1,000. Since the standard deduction for Bill is $5,700, he should not itemize his deductions. This means he does not get to deduct any of his gambling losses.

EXAMPLE 2: Last year Jill, a single taxpayer, or had $12,000 in gambling losses and $10,000 in winnings. Like Bill, Jill ordinarily doesn't itemize her deductions. But, when she adds her deductible $10,000 gambling loss to her other itemized deductions, she has a total of $13,000 in itemized deductions. Clearly, she should itemize this year because her itemized deductions exceed the $5,700 standard deduction. Jill will report the $10,000 in winnings as income on her return and list $10,000 of her $12,000 loss as an itemized deduction. The remaining $2,000 in losses is not deductible at all, ever.

# Step 4: Fill Out Your Tax Return

Filling out your return for your gambling wins and losses is relatively easy. You have to use IRS Form 1040; you can't use any of the shorter IRS tax forms such as Form 1040-EZ.

### List total winnings on 1040

List the total of all your winning gambling sessions for the year on Line 21 of your Form 1040. This line is titled "Other income." Write "Gambling winnings" on the dotted line, and then enter the amount in the line 21 column.

You add the amount in line 21 to all your other income for the year and include the total in line 22. This is your total income for the year. Thus, your gambling winnings are included in your total income regardless of how much you lost. Even if you lost more than you won, you must include your total winnings in your income. This can have extremely harsh tax consequences (see below).

 Do You Use TurboTax?

Do you use TurboTax to do your taxes? If so, you should be aware that the way it calculates your total gambling winnings can cause you to report more winnings than you actually had. The way TurboTax works is to first ask you to list the total winnings reported on your Forms W-2G, if any. Then, you separately list the total winnings not reported on Form W-2G. These two numbers are automatically added together to arrive at your total annual winnings. This is not how you're supposed to determine your annual winnings. As explained above, your winnings are supposed to be calculated by adding up all your winning gambling sessions for the year, not by adding the amounts on your W-2Gs. Since the winnings reported on any Form W-2G could well have been lost before the session ended, doing it the TurboTax way will likely inflate your winnings.

### List gambling tax withholding on Form 1040

If you had any tax withheld from your winnings during the year, add the total amount to your other taxes withheld, such as those withheld from your salary by your employer and reported on your IRS Form W-2. List the total tax withheld on line 61 of Form 1040.

Tax withholdings from your gambling winnings should be shown on the Form W-2Gs issued to you by casinos or other gambling establishments. Be sure to attach copies of these Form W-2Gs to your Form 1040. You only need to attach the W-2Gs that show taxes withheld.

### List losses on Schedule A

If you elect to itemize your deductions, you file Schedule A with your return and list your itemized deductions there. If you don't itemize, don't file Schedule A—you get no deduction for your gambling losses.

Itemizers are allowed to deduct their gambling losses up to the amount of their winnings. List your total losses—up to the amount of your winnings—on line 28 of Schedule A, titled "Other Miscellaneous Deductions." Write "Gambling losses" on the dotted line, followed by the amount in the line 28 column.

Make absolutely sure *not* to list your gambling losses in line 23, which is called "Other expenses." All the expenses listed here are subject to a 2% of AGI limitation—that is, they are deductible only to the extent they exceed 2% of your Adjusted Gross Income (see below). Gambling losses are not subject to this limitation and do not belong on this line.

Your gambling losses are added to all your other itemized deductions and the total subtracted from your adjusted gross income. Thus, although your winnings and losses are kept separate on your return, itemizers' losses end up reducing the amount of their taxable income and thereby offset all or part of their winnings.

### Sample tax return

Here is a sample tax return for a recreational gambler who won $10,000 and lost $12,000 in 2010. He also had $2,000 in tax withheld from his winnings by the casino, along with $8,000 in payroll tax withholding by his employer. He elects to itemize his personal deductions and files Schedule A with his return.

| Form **1040** | Department of the Treasury—Internal Revenue Service **U.S. Individual Income Tax Return** **2010** | | (99) | IRS Use Only—Do not write or staple in this space. | |
|---|---|---|---|---|---|
| | For the year Jan. 1–Dec. 31, 2010, or other tax year beginning | , 2010, ending | , 20 | OMB No. 1545-0074 | |

**Name, Address, and SSN**

See separate instructions.

| Your first name and initial | Last name | Your social security number |
|---|---|---|
| John | Jones | 123456789 |
| If a joint return, spouse's first name and initial | Last name | Spouse's social security number |
| Home address (number and street). If you have a P.O. box, see instructions. 123 Main St. | | Apt. no. | ▲ Make sure the SSN(s) above and on line 6c are correct. |
| City, town or post office, state, and ZIP code. If you have a foreign address, see instructions. Anytown, CA 90000 | | | Checking a box below will not change your tax or refund. |

**Presidential Election Campaign** ► Check here if you, or your spouse if filing jointly, want $3 to go to this fund . . ► ☐ You ☐ Spouse

**Filing Status**

Check only one box.

1 ☑ Single
2 ☐ Married filing jointly (even if only one had income)
3 ☐ Married filing separately. Enter spouse's SSN above and full name here. ►
4 ☐ Head of household (with qualifying person). (See instructions.) If the qualifying person is a child but not your dependent, enter this child's name here. ►
5 ☐ Qualifying widow(er) with dependent child

**Exemptions**

If more than four dependents, see instructions and check here ► ☐

| 6a ☑ Yourself. If someone can claim you as a dependent, do not check box 6a | | | | Boxes checked on 6a and 6b | 1 |
|---|---|---|---|---|---|
| b ☐ Spouse | | | | No. of children on 6c who: | |
| c Dependents: (1) First name  Last name | (2) Dependent's social security number | (3) Dependent's relationship to you | (4) ✓ if child under age 17 qualifying for child tax credit (see page 15) | • lived with you • did not live with you due to divorce or separation (see instructions) Dependents on 6c not entered above | |
| | | | ☐ | | |
| | | | ☐ | | |
| | | | ☐ | | |
| | | | ☐ | | |
| d Total number of exemptions claimed . . . . . . . | | | Add numbers on lines above ► | 1 |

**Income**

Attach Form(s) W-2 here. Also attach Forms W-2G and 1099-R if tax was withheld.

If you did not get a W-2, see page 20.

Enclose, but do not attach, any payment. Also, please use Form 1040-V.

| 7 | Wages, salaries, tips, etc. Attach Form(s) W-2 . . . . . . . | 7 | 50,000 |
|---|---|---|---|
| 8a | Taxable interest. Attach Schedule B if required . . . . . . . | 8a | |
| b | Tax-exempt interest. Do not include on line 8a . . . | 8b | |
| 9a | Ordinary dividends. Attach Schedule B if required . . . . . . | 9a | |
| b | Qualified dividends . . . . . . . | 9b | |
| 10 | Taxable refunds, credits, or offsets of state and local income taxes | 10 | |
| 11 | Alimony received . . . . . . . | 11 | |
| 12 | Business income or (loss). Attach Schedule C or C-EZ . . . . | 12 | |
| 13 | Capital gain or (loss). Attach Schedule D if required. If not required, check here ► ☐ | 13 | |
| 14 | Other gains or (losses). Attach Form 4797 . . . . . | 14 | |
| 15a | IRA distributions 15a | b Taxable amount | 15b | |
| 16a | Pensions and annuities 16a | b Taxable amount | 16b | |
| 17 | Rental real estate, royalties, partnerships, S corporations, trusts, etc. Attach Schedule E | 17 | |
| 18 | Farm income or (loss). Attach Schedule F . . . . . . | 18 | |
| 19 | Unemployment compensation . . . . . . | 19 | |
| 20a | Social security benefits 20a | b Taxable amount | 20b | |
| 21 | Other income. List type and amount Gambling winnings | 21 | 10,000 |
| 22 | Combine the amounts in the far right column for lines 7 through 21. This is your total income ► | 22 | |

**Adjusted Gross Income**

| 23 | Educator expenses . . . . . . | 23 | |
|---|---|---|---|
| 24 | Certain business expenses of reservists, performing artists, and fee-basis government officials. Attach Form 2106 or 2106-EZ | 24 | |
| 25 | Health savings account deduction. Attach Form 8889 . | 25 | |
| 26 | Moving expenses. Attach Form 3903 . . . | 26 | |
| 27 | One-half of self-employment tax. Attach Schedule SE . | 27 | |
| 28 | Self-employed SEP, SIMPLE, and qualified plans . | 28 | |
| 29 | Self-employed health insurance deduction . . | 29 | |
| 30 | Penalty on early withdrawal of savings . . . | 30 | |
| 31a | Alimony paid  b Recipient's SSN ► | 31a | |
| 32 | IRA deduction . . . . . . | 32 | |
| 33 | Student loan interest deduction . . . | 33 | |
| 34 | Tuition and fees. Attach Form 8917 . . . . | 34 | |
| 35 | Domestic production activities deduction. Attach Form 8903 | 35 | |
| 36 | Add lines 23 through 31a and 32 through 35 . . . . . . ► | 36 | |
| 37 | Subtract line 36 from line 22. This is your adjusted gross income . . . ► | 37 | 60,000 |

For Disclosure, Privacy Act, and Paperwork Reduction Act Notice, see separate instructions. Cat. No. 11320B Form **1040** (2010)

Form 1040 (2010)
Page **2**

| | | | | | |
|---|---|---|---|---|---|
| **Tax and Credits** | 38 | Amount from line 37 (adjusted gross income) | | 38 | 60,000 |
| | 39a | Check { ☐ You were born before January 2, 1946, ☐ Blind. } Total boxes ☐ Spouse was born before January 2, 1946, ☐ Blind. checked ▶ 39a ☐ | | | |
| | b | If your spouse itemizes on a separate return or you were a dual-status alien, check here ▶ 39b ☐ | | | |
| | 40 | **Itemized deductions** (from Schedule A) or your **standard deduction** (see instructions) | | 40 | 15,000 |
| | 41 | Subtract line 40 from line 38 | | 41 | 45,000 |
| | 42 | **Exemptions.** Multiply $3,650 by the number on line 6d | | 42 | 3,650 |
| | 43 | **Taxable income.** Subtract line 42 from line 41. If line 42 is more than line 41, enter -0- | | 43 | 41,350 |
| | 44 | **Tax** (see instructions). Check if any tax is from: a ☐ Form(s) 8814 b ☐ Form 4972 | | 44 | 6,510 |
| | 45 | **Alternative minimum tax** (see instructions). Attach Form 6251 | | 45 | |
| | 46 | Add lines 44 and 45 | ▶ | 46 | 6,510 |
| | 47 | Foreign tax credit. Attach Form 1116 if required | 47 | | |
| | 48 | Credit for child and dependent care expenses. Attach Form 2441 | 48 | | |
| | 49 | Education credits from Form 8863, line 23 | 49 | | |
| | 50 | Retirement savings contributions credit. Attach Form 8880 | 50 | | |
| | 51 | Child tax credit (see instructions) | 51 | | |
| | 52 | Residential energy credits. Attach Form 5695 | 52 | | |
| | 53 | Other credits from Form: a ☐ 3800 b ☐ 8801 c ☐ | 53 | | |
| | 54 | Add lines 47 through 53. These are your **total credits** | | 54 | |
| | 55 | Subtract line 54 from line 46. If line 54 is more than line 46, enter -0- | ▶ | 55 | 6,510 |
| **Other Taxes** | 56 | Self-employment tax. Attach Schedule SE | | 56 | |
| | 57 | Unreported social security and Medicare tax from Form: a ☐ 4137 b ☐ 8919 | | 57 | |
| | 58 | Additional tax on IRAs, other qualified retirement plans, etc. Attach Form 5329 if required | | 58 | |
| | 59 | a ☐ Form(s) W-2, box 9 b ☐ Schedule H c ☐ Form 5405, line 16 | | 59 | |
| | 60 | Add lines 55 through 59. This is your **total tax** | ▶ | 60 | |
| **Payments** | 61 | Federal income tax withheld from Forms W-2 and 1099 | 61 | | |
| | 62 | 2010 estimated tax payments and amount applied from 2009 return | 62 | | |
| If you have a qualifying child, attach Schedule EIC. | 63 | Making work pay credit. Attach Schedule M | 63 | | |
| | 64a | **Earned income credit (EIC)** | 64a | | |
| | b | Nontaxable combat pay election 64b | | | |
| | 65 | Additional child tax credit. Attach Form 8812 | 65 | | |
| | 66 | American opportunity credit from Form 8863, line 14 | 66 | | |
| | 67 | First-time homebuyer credit from Form 5405, line 10 | 67 | | |
| | 68 | Amount paid with request for extension to file | 68 | | |
| | 69 | Excess social security and tier 1 RRTA tax withheld | 69 | | |
| | 70 | Credit for federal tax on fuels. Attach Form 4136 | 70 | | |
| | 71 | Credits from Form: a ☐ 2439 b ☐ 8839 c ☐ 8801 d ☐ 8885 | 71 | | |
| | 72 | Add lines 61, 62, 63, 64a, and 65 through 71. These are your **total payments** | ▶ | 72 | 10,000 |
| **Refund** | 73 | If line 72 is more than line 60, subtract line 60 from line 72. This is the amount you **overpaid** | | 73 | 3,481 |
| | 74a | Amount of line 73 you want **refunded to you.** If Form 8888 is attached, check here ▶ ☐ | | 74a | 3,481 |
| Direct deposit? ▶ See instructions. | b | Routing number ▶ c Type: ☐ Checking ☐ Savings | | | |
| | d | Account number | | | |
| | 75 | Amount of line 73 you want applied to your 2011 estimated tax ▶ 75 | | | |
| **Amount You Owe** | 76 | **Amount you owe.** Subtract line 72 from line 60. For details on how to pay, see instructions ▶ | | 76 | |
| | 77 | Estimated tax penalty (see instructions) 77 | | | |
| **Third Party Designee** | | Do you want to allow another person to discuss this return with the IRS (see instructions)? ☐ Yes. Complete below. ☐ No | | | |
| | | Designee's name ▶ Phone no. ▶ Personal identification number (PIN) ▶ | | | |

**Sign Here**
Joint return?
See page 12.
Keep a copy for your records.

Under penalties of perjury, I declare that I have examined this return and accompanying schedules and statements, and to the best of my knowledge and belief, they are true, correct, and complete. Declaration of preparer (other than taxpayer) is based on all information of which preparer has any knowledge.

| Your signature | Date | Your occupation | Daytime phone number |
|---|---|---|---|
| | | Steve008 | 123 456-7890 |
| Spouse's signature. If a joint return, both must sign. | Date | Spouse's occupation | |

**Paid Preparer Use Only**

| Print/Type preparer's name | Preparer's signature | Date | Check ☐ if self-employed | PTIN |
|---|---|---|---|---|
| Firm's name ▶ | | | Firm's EIN ▶ | |
| Firm's address ▶ | | | Phone no. | |

Form **1040** (2010)

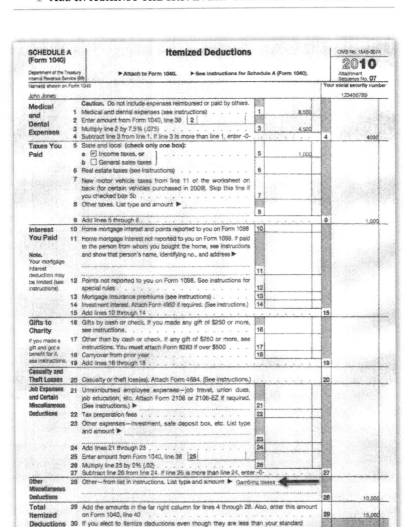

| SCHEDULE A (Form 1040) | | Itemized Deductions | OMB No. 1545-0074 2010 |
|---|---|---|---|
| Department of the Treasury Internal Revenue Service (99) | ► Attach to Form 1040.  ► See Instructions for Schedule A (Form 1040). | | Attachment Sequence No. 07 |
| Name(s) shown on Form 1040 | | | Your social security number |
| John Jones | | | 123456789 |

| | | | | | | | | | |
|---|---|---|---|---|---|---|---|---|---|
| **Medical and Dental Expenses** | | Caution. Do not include expenses reimbursed or paid by others. | | | | | | | |
| | 1 | Medical and dental expenses (see instructions) | | 1 | 8,500 | | | | |
| | 2 | Enter amount from Form 1040, line 38 | 2 | | | | | | |
| | 3 | Multiply line 2 by 7.5% (.075) | | 3 | 4,500 | | | | |
| | 4 | Subtract line 3 from line 1. If line 3 is more than line 1, enter -0- | | | | | 4 | 4000 | |
| **Taxes You Paid** | 5 | State and local (check only one box): | | | | | | | |
| | | a ☑ Income taxes, or | | 5 | 1,000 | | | | |
| | | b ☐ General sales taxes | | | | | | | |
| | 6 | Real estate taxes (see instructions) | | 6 | | | | | |
| | 7 | New motor vehicle taxes from line 11 of the worksheet on back (for certain vehicles purchased in 2009). Skip this line if you checked box 5b | | 7 | | | | | |
| | 8 | Other taxes. List type and amount ► _____ | | 8 | | | | | |
| | 9 | Add lines 5 through 8 | | | | | 9 | 1,000 | |
| **Interest You Paid** | 10 | Home mortgage interest and points reported to you on Form 1098 | 10 | | | | | | |
| | 11 | Home mortgage interest not reported to you on Form 1098. If paid to the person from whom you bought the home, see instructions and show that person's name, identifying no., and address ► | | | | | | | |
| **Note.** Your mortgage interest deduction may be limited (see instructions). | | _____ | 11 | | | | | | |
| | 12 | Points not reported to you on Form 1098. See instructions for special rules | 12 | | | | | | |
| | 13 | Mortgage insurance premiums (see instructions) | 13 | | | | | | |
| | 14 | Investment interest. Attach Form 4952 if required. (See instructions.) | 14 | | | | | | |
| | 15 | Add lines 10 through 14 | | | | | 15 | | |
| **Gifts to Charity** | 16 | Gifts by cash or check. If you made any gift of $250 or more, see instructions. | 16 | | | | | | |
| If you made a gift and got a benefit for it, see instructions. | 17 | Other than by cash or check. If any gift of $250 or more, see instructions. You must attach Form 8283 if over $500 | 17 | | | | | | |
| | 18 | Carryover from prior year | 18 | | | | | | |
| | 19 | Add lines 16 through 18 | | | | | 19 | | |
| **Casualty and Theft Losses** | 20 | Casualty or theft loss(es). Attach Form 4684. (See instructions.) | | | | | 20 | | |
| **Job Expenses and Certain Miscellaneous Deductions** | 21 | Unreimbursed employee expenses—job travel, union dues, job education, etc. Attach Form 2106 or 2106-EZ if required. (See instructions.) ► | 21 | | | | | | |
| | 22 | Tax preparation fees | 22 | | | | | | |
| | 23 | Other expenses—investment, safe deposit box, etc. List type and amount ► _____ | 23 | | | | | | |
| | 24 | Add lines 21 through 23 | 24 | | | | | | |
| | 25 | Enter amount from Form 1040, line 38 | 25 | | | | | | |
| | 26 | Multiply line 25 by 2% (.02) | 26 | | | | | | |
| | 27 | Subtract line 26 from line 24. If line 26 is more than line 24, enter -0- | | | | | 27 | | |
| **Other Miscellaneous Deductions** | 28 | Other—from list in instructions. List type and amount ► Gambling losses ◄ | | | | | 28 | 10,000 | |
| **Total Itemized Deductions** | 29 | Add the amounts in the far right column for lines 4 through 28. Also, enter this amount on Form 1040, line 40 | | | | | 29 | 15,000 | |
| | 30 | If you elect to itemize deductions even though they are less than your standard deduction, check here ► ☐ | | | | | | | |

| For Paperwork Reduction Act Notice, see Form 1040 instructions. | Cat. No. 17145C | Schedule A (Form 1040) 2010 |
|---|---|---|

# Are Your Wins Less than Your Form W-2Gs?

A common problem gamblers face is that their actual wins for the year are less than the total wins reported to the IRS on Form W-2Gs by casinos. This can happen because Form W-2Gs are based on the results of one spin, hand, or play. They are not based on what you won or lost during an entire gambling session. Before a session ends, you can end up losing all the money listed on the W-2G sent to the IRS. The IRS itself recognizes this fact.

> *EXAMPLE: Bill is an avid slot player—that's all he plays. On September 1, Bill walked into the Pair-a-Dice casino with $100 in his pocket. He played the slots and quickly won a $5,000 jackpot. The casino issued Bill a Form W-2G reporting the big win to the IRS. Bill took his $5,000 and continued to play the slots. Unfortunately, by the end of the day he lost all his winnings plus the $100 he started with. As far as Bill is concerned, he lost $100 for that one-day gambling session. When he does his taxes, he'll add that $100 loss to his other losses for the year. The $5,000 jackpot will not be included in his winnings, since he lost it all by the end of the gambling session. When he totals all his winning sessions for the year, he ends up with $1,000 in winnings, and lists that amount as his gambling income. Unfortunately, the IRS doesn't know that Bill lost the $5,000 jackpot. All it knows is that Bill won $5,000 on September 1. When it sees $1,000 in gambling income on Bill's return instead of $5,000, it notes the discrepancy and flags Bill's return for further review.*

What should you do if your Form W-2Gs overstate your winnings? There is no single, clear answer. This is largely because the IRS is not consistent in the way it deals with this issue.

One approach is simply to make sure that your total winnings are at least as much as the totals of all your Form W-2Gs, even if this is more than your winnings on a per-session basis. This avoids having the IRS computer flag your return for review. If you have enough losses to offset your winnings, you won't owe any tax on the winnings. However, your adjusted gross income will be higher than it otherwise would be, and this could cost you valuable deductions (see the following section.)

Another approach is to only report your per-session winnings, even though this amount is lower than the total of your Form W-2Gs. You should attach a separate schedule to your return listing each Form W-2G you received along with its amount. Add the following note: "The amounts listed above are included in the gambling winnings reported in Form 1040, line 21." It's likely that your return will be flagged for review and the IRS may send you a deficiency notice demanding that you pay tax on the additional winnings reported in the W-2Gs. For this reason, you should have immaculate, accurate records backing up the amounts you claim to have won and lost during each gambling session. You'll need to explain to the IRS that you calculated your wins and losses correctly and have good records. This may take a few letters or phone calls, but in the end the IRS will probably let the matter drop if you have good records.

If you have very substantial gambling winnings reported on Forms W-2Gs, you may want to consult with a tax pro before deciding what to do.

# Effect of Gambling Wins On Your Tax Deductions

The tax laws can be incredibly cruel when it comes to gambling. Because of they unfair way they work, it's possible for a person who lost more than he won to owe extra taxes. In effect, gamblers are being punished just for the act of gambling. No one else is treated this way by the tax law.

## You lose itemized deductions

Here's what can happen: as explained above, you have to report all your gambling winnings as "other income" on your Form 1040. This "other income" is added to your adjusted gross income (AGI). Your AGI is your total income minus a handful of specified deductions, such as business expenses. Your gambling losses are not one of these deductions for AGI.

The amount of your AGI is very important because literally dozens of tax deductions are limited to the amount they exceed a specified percentage of your AGI. The higher your AGI, the less you can deduct. For example:

- *Medical expenses*: You can deduct only the amount of your unreimbursed medical expenses that is more than 7.5% of your AGI. For example, if you have an AGI of $100,000, you can only deduct the amount of your unreimbursed medical expenses that exceed $7,500 (7.5% of $100,000).
- *Miscellaneous itemized deductions*: These deductions are subject to a 2% of AGI floor—that is, you can only deduct the amount that exceeds 2% of your adjusted gross income. Miscellaneous itemized deductions include unreimbursed

employee expenses, investment expenses, fees paid to tax preparers, union dues, professional association dues, job-related clothing or equipment, subscriptions related to your job, expenses of looking for a new job, work-related educational expenses, and home office expenses.

*Example: Karen had $25,000 in unreimbursed medical expenses this year. If Karen didn't gamble, her AGI would be $50,000. Since 7.5% of $50,000 is $3,750, Karen could deduct $21,250 of her medical expenses as an itemized deduction. However, Karen won $50,000 from gambling and lost even more. Karen must add her winnings to her AGI, pushing it to $100,000. Because 7.5% of $100,000 is $7,500, Karen may deduct only $17,500 of her medical expenses instead of $21,250. Thus, Karen ends up paying an additional $375 in income taxes.*

### Your Social Security benefits may be taxable

If you receive Social Security, adding your gambling income to your AGI may also result in you having to pay income tax on your benefits. For example, if you're single, you have to pay income tax on up to 50% of your benefits if your "combined income" is between $25,000 and $34,000. If you're single and your combined income is over $34,000, up to 85% of your benefits are taxable. Your combined income includes your AGI, which includes your gambling losses. Thus, if you have substantial gambling winnings, your AGI may pass the income tax threshold.

*Example: Bill, a retired single, receives $20,000 in Social Security benefits each year and has $5,000 in other income. An avid* *gambler, Bill won $20,000 and lost $25,000 during the year. He must add the $20,000 in winnings to his AGI. This puts his "combined income" over $34,000. As a result, he must pay income tax on 85% of his benefits. This is so even though he lost $5,000 from gambling!*

### You may not qualify for tax credits and other benefits

Eligibility for certain tax credits and other benefits is based on the amount of the taxpayer's AGI. If AGI is too high, such benefits may be reduced or eliminated. In one actual case, for example, a woman with $11,835 in wage income was entitled to receive the earned income tax credit—a credit designed to help poor people. Unfortunately, she also won $9,180 gambling during the year, and lost at least that much. The IRS added the $9,180 in winnings to her AGI and, as a result, her tax credit was reduced from $3,888 to $1,755. (Petty v. Comm'r, T.C. Memo 2004-144 (2004).)

# chapter 7

# State Income Taxes

Paying federal income tax on your gambling winnings is bad enough; but, to add insult to injury, 41 states impose their own income taxes on gambling income. If you live in one of these states, you could end up with a state, as well as federal, tax bill on your winnings. Moreover, if you gamble out-of-state, you could owe income taxes in that state as well.

Unfortunately, the states don't all tax gambling the same way. Most follow the federal tax law, but some don't. In fact, you could owe income tax on your winnings in some states even though you owe no federal tax on the money.

The rules covered here apply only to casual gamblers. Professional gamblers are not subject to them. A person who qualifies as a professional gambler is taxed like any other small business. See Chapter 8 for more information on professional gambler status.

For more information on your state's taxes, refer to your state tax agency's website. Links to tax sites for all 50 states can be found at: http://www.taxsites.com/State-Links.html

# Income Taxes In Your Home State

First, if your home state (the state in which you live) has income taxes, you'll have to pay the applicable state tax on all your gambling income, wherever it was won. Whether and how much income tax you could have to pay depends on the state you live in.

### States that don't tax gambling

The following states have no income taxes; thus, they don't tax gambling income. These are:

- Alaska
- Florida
- Nevada
- South Dakota
- Texas
- Washington
- Wyoming.

Tennessee imposes income tax only on investment and dividend income, so it doesn't tax gambling income either.

If you live in any of these states, you don't have to worry about paying state income tax on your gambling income.

### States that track federal tax law

In most states, the amount of state income tax you must pay is based on your federal income tax. These states use your federal adjusted gross income (AGI) as the starting point to compute your state tax, and also allow all or most of the federal itemized deductions. These states treat your gambling winnings and losses the same as the IRS: If you're a casual gambler, your total winnings are added to your state AGI and your losses deducted as a state itemized deduction. If you don't itemize, you get no deduction. However, some states don't tax state lottery winnings.

*Example: Frank lives in Colorado. Last year he had $10,000 in gambling income and $5,000 in losses. When he does his federal taxes, he adds his $10,000 in winnings to his AGI. He itemizes his deductions on his federal return and includes his $5,000 loss in this amount. He had $15,000 in non-gambling itemized deductions, so his total federal itemized deductions are $20,000. When he does his Colorado income taxes, he uses these exact same numbers. The Colorado income tax rate is 4.63%. Thus, Frank ends up paying $231 in state income tax on his $5,000 of taxable winnings.*

The states that follow the Feds are:

- Alabama
- Arizona (up to $5,000 in state lottery winnings tax exempt)

- Arkansas
- California (state lottery winnings tax exempt)
- Colorado
- Delaware (state lottery winnings tax exempt)
- Georgia
- Hawaii
- Idaho (state lottery winnings tax exempt)
- Iowa
- Kansas
- Kentucky
- Maine
- Maryland
- Minnesota
- Missouri
- Montana
- Nebraska
- New Jersey (state lottery winnings tax exempt)
- New Mexico
- New York
- North Carolina
- North Dakota
- Oklahoma
- Oregon (state lottery winnings of $600 or less from a single ticket or play are tax exempt).
- Pennsylvania (state lottery winnings and comps from PA casinos tax exempt)
- Rhode Island
- South Carolina
- Utah

- Vermont
- Virginia.

## Problem states

Unfortunately, there are 14 states that don't follow federal tax law for gambling winnings. In most of these states, gambling losses claimed as itemized deductions on a federal return are *not allowed* on the state income tax return. This means that you'll owe income tax on your winnings even if you lost more than you won during the year! A true tax nightmare.

*Example: Jane lives in Illinois, which does not allow any deduction for gambling losses. Last year she won $100,000 gambling and lost $150,000. She gets a $100,000 itemized deduction for her losses on her federal return. But she gets no deduction for her losses on her state return. This means she must pay the Illinois income tax on all of her $100,000 winnings, even though she lost more than that amount. Illinois has a 5% income tax, so Jane must pay an extra $3,000.*

If you live in one of these states, and you truthfully report all your winnings, as you are required to, you may not be able to gamble as much as you'd like because of the added tax burden it brings.

The states that don't allow gambling losses to be deducted include:

- **Connecticut:** No deduction allowed for gambling losses. State income tax must be paid on gambling winnings if residents' gross income exceeds specified limits.

- **Illinois:** No deduction allowed for gambling losses.
- **Indiana:** No deduction allowed for gambling losses.
- **Louisiana:** No deduction allowed for gambling losses.
- **Massachusetts:** Gambling losses are not deductible
- **Michigan:** Gambling losses are not deductible. However, Michigan residents may exclude from their taxable income the first $300 won from gambling, bingo, awards or prizes.
- **Ohio:** No deduction is allowed for gambling losses through the end of 2012. Beginning with tax year 2013, Ohio residents will be able to deduct gambling losses up to the amount of their winnings.
- **Wisconsin:** No deduction allowed for gambling losses. However, a tax credit is allowed based on certain federal itemized deductions reported on federal Schedule A (not including gambling losses).

A few other states have different rules on how gambling income is taxed:

- **Minnesota:** Gambling losses are allowed for regular income tax purposes, but they are not allowed in determining the Minnesota Alternative Minimum Tax. If you claimed gambling losses on federal Schedule A and the total of your federal itemized deductions and personal and dependent exemption amounts exceeds $66,490 for a married couple filing jointly, or $49,860 for a single or head of household, there is a good chance you will be subject to the Minnesota AMT.
- **Mississippi:** Winnings and losses from casinos outside

Mississippi are treated the same as under federal tax law. However, gambling winnings reported on IRS Form W-2G, 1099, or other informational return from Mississippi casinos are subject to a 3% non-refundable income tax. The casinos withhold the tax at the time of payout. Mississippi residents need not include such winnings in their Mississippi income.

• **New Hampshire**: A 10% flat tax is imposed on all gambling winnings.

# Income Tax Outside Your Home State

Do you have to pay state income taxes in a state where you gamble, but don't live? For example, if you live in Nevada and gamble at a race track in California, do you have to pay California income taxes on your winnings?

As a general rule, the answer is "yes." Most states that have an income tax require nonresidents to pay state tax on gambling winnings won at casinos or other gambling establishments located within the state. The money is taxed at the state's out-of-state income tax rate. The casino may also be required to withhold state income tax from your winnings.

Be aware that, if an IRS Form W-2G is filed, a copy must be sent to the state in which the money was won. In this event, the state tax agency will be expecting you to file a nonresident income tax return reporting the money you won in the state. On the other hand, people who don't win enough to have a Form W-2G issued or state taxes withheld, rarely bother to file a nonresident return, and states rarely go after them.

Fortunately, most states that have income taxes provide tax credits to their residents to offset income taxes they pay in other states. If your home state has the same or lower tax rate as the state where you won the money, you won't owe anything else to your home state on those winnings. But if your home state has a higher tax rate, you'll have to pay the difference to your home state.

To obtain such a credit, you must file a nonresident tax return in the state where you won the money. On this return, report only your gambling winnings from that state, and any amount withheld. When you file your return for your home state, report all your gambling income, including all your out-of-state winnings. You then claim a credit on your state return to offset the tax you paid on the out-of-state winnings.

Other states don't offer such credits. However, you may be able to obtain a refund of taxes withheld by a state where you don't live by filing a nonresident tax return. The rules on how much of a refund you can get differ from state-to-state.

Contact your state tax agency for details. You can find a list of all state tax agencies at http://www.taxsites.com/State-Links.html

# State Tax Withholding

Most states that tax gambling require state income tax withheld from winnings earned by gamblers while gambling in the state if federal tax is withheld (see Chapter 3 for a detailed discussion of federal tax withholding). Such withholding is usually required whether or not you are a resident of the state involved. State withholding rates vary from state-to-state, as shown in the chart below. If too much is withheld, you can get a refund by filing a nonresident income tax return with the state.

| State Tax Treatment of Gambling | | | | | |
|---|---|---|---|---|---|
| State | Income Taxes Imposed? | Gambling Losses Deductible? | State Income Tax Rates | Income Tax Withholding Rates | Special Rules |
| Alabama | Yes | Yes | 2%-5% | | |
| Alaska | No | | | | |
| Arizona | Yes | Yes | 2.59%-4.54% | 5% (6% for nonresidents) | Up to $5,000 in lottery winnings tax exempt |
| Arkansas | Yes | Yes | 1%-7% | | |
| California | Yes | Yes | 1.25%-9.55% | 7% (no withholding on lottery winnings) | State lottery winnings tax exempt |
| Colorado | Yes | | 4.63% | 4% | |
| Connecticut | Yes | No | 3%-6.5% | 6.5% | Gross income must exceed threshold amount for winnings to be taxable |

| State Tax Treatment of Gambling | | | | | |
|---|---|---|---|---|---|
| State | Income Taxes Imposed? | Gambling Losses Deductible? | State Income Tax Rates | Income Tax Withholding Rates | Special Rules |
| Delaware | Delaware | Yes | 2.2%-6.95% | | State lottery winnings tax exempt |
| Florida | No | | | | |
| Georgia | Yes | Yes | 1%-6% | 6% | |
| Hawaii | Yes | Yes | 1.4%-11% | | |
| Idaho | Yes | Yes | 1.6%-7.8% | 7.8% | State lottery winnings tax exempt |
| Illinois | Yes | No | 5% | 5% | |
| Indiana | Yes | No | 3.4% | 3.4% | |
| Iowa | Yes | Yes | 0.36%-8.98% | 5% | |
| Kansas | Yes | Yes | 3.5%-6.45% | 5% | |
| Kentucky | Yes | Yes | 2%-6% | 6% | |
| Louisiana | Yes | No | 2%-6% | | |
| Maine | Yes | Yes | 2%-8.5% | 5% | |
| Maryland | Yes | Yes | 2%-6.25% | 9.25% (7.5% for nonresidents) | |
| Massachusetts | Yes | No | 5.3% | 5% | |
| Michigan | Yes | No | 4.35% | 4.35% | First $300 won tax exempt |
| Minnesota | Yes | Yes | 5.35%-7.85% | 7.25% | Losses not allowed to determine state alternative minimum tax |

| | State Tax Treatment of Gambling | | | | |
|---|---|---|---|---|---|
| **State** | **Income Taxes Imposed?** | **Gambling Losses Deductible?** | **State Income Tax Rates** | **Income Tax Withholding Rates** | **Special Rules** |
| Mississippi | Yes | Yes | 3%-5% | 3% (not refundable) | 3% flat tax on casino winnings |
| Missouri | Yes | Yes | 1.5%-6% | 4% | |
| Montana | Yes | Yes | 1%-6.9% | 10% | |
| Nebraska | Yes | Yes | 2.56%-6.84% | 5% | |
| Nevada | No | | | | |
| New Hampshire | No | | | 10% | 10% tax on all winnings |
| New Jersey | Yes | Yes | 1.4%-10.75% | 10.8% | State lottery winnings tax exempt |
| New Mexico | Yes | Yes | 1.7%-4.9% | 6% | |
| New York | Yes | Yes | 4%-8.97% | 8.97% (plus 3.678% for New York City residents) | |
| North Carolina | Yes | Yes | 6%-7.75% | 7% | |
| North Dakota | Yes | Yes | 1.84%-4.86% | 5.54% | |
| Ohio | Yes | No | 0.618%-6.24% | 6% | |
| Oklahoma | Yes | Yes | 0.5%-5.50% | 4% | |
| Oregon | Yes | Yes | 5%-11% | 8% | State lottery winnings up to $600 tax exempt |

| State Tax Treatment of Gambling | | | | | |
|---|---|---|---|---|---|
| State | Income Taxes Imposed? | Gambling Losses Deductible? | State Income Tax Rates | Income Tax Withholding Rates | Special Rules |
| Pennsylvania | Yes | Yes | 3.07% | | State lottery winnings tax exempt |
| Rhode Island | Yes | Yes | 3.8%-9.9% | 7% | |
| South Carolina | Yes | Yes | 0%-7% | 7% | |
| South Dakota | No | | | | |
| Tennessee | No | | | | |
| Texas | No | | | | |
| Utah | Yes | Yes | 5% | | |
| Vermont | Yes | Yes | 3.55%-8.95% | 6% | |
| Virginia | Yes | Yes | 2%-5.75% | 4% | |
| Washington | No | | | | |
| West Virginia | Yes | No | | 6.5% | |
| Wisconsin | Yes | No | | 7.75% | |
| Wyoming | No | | | | |

# Tax Rules for
# Professional Gamblers

Are you (or do you want to be) a professional gambler? If so, this chapter is for you. The tax rules for professional gamblers are vastly different than those that apply to casual or recreational gamblers. Professional gamblers get many tax deductions and other tax breaks that recreational gamblers don't have. As a result, professional gamblers often pay less tax on their winnings than casual gamblers. But this isn't always true.

The IRS has always been hostile toward people who claim to be professional gamblers. If you claim to be one, it's likely your tax return will be given extra scrutiny. If the IRS audits your taxes and concludes you're not really a professional, you could end up owing back taxes, interest, and penalties. Thus, you need to make sure you qualify as a gambling professional before you file your taxes as one. If you're unsure whether you qualify, consult a tax professional for advice.

# Are You Really a Professional Gambler?

Simply claiming to be a professional gambler doesn't make you one in the eys of the IRS. To be a professional gambler for tax purposes, your gambling activity must be a bona fide business, not something you do for recreation, as a hobby, or because you are addicted to gambling. Few people can qualify as professional gamblers. Indeed, until 1987, the IRS said there was no such thing as a professional gambler. However, that year the United States Supreme Court said that gambling can qualify as a business if it is pursued regularly and continuously with the objective of earning a profit.(*Commissioner v. Groetzinger,* 480 U.S. 23, 35 (1987).) Thus, there are two separate requirements you must meet to be a gambling pro:

- your gambling activities must be continuous and regular, and
- you must gamble primarily to earn a profit.

### Continuous and regular test

The IRS and most courts say that to be a professional gambler you must gamble full-time—that is, you must gamble at least as often as a person typically works at a regular job. Part-time or sporadic gambling won't cut it.

Here are examples of the amounts of time put in by gamblers who passed the test:

- 40 hours per week handicapping and betting on horse races, spending more than 250 days at the race track each year
- 60 to 80 hours per week attending and betting on dog races six days a week
- 35 hours every week betting at the race track
- gambling at casinos for 176 days during one year
- betting at the race track six days a week for 48 weeks during the year.

Here are examples of people who didn't put in enough time to pass the test:

- playing slot machines at Iowa casinos for approximately 66 days during the 274-day period from January to September
- playing the slot machines in a local casino 20 to 25 hours per week
- gambling at casinos for 43 days during one year
- gambling at various North Dakota casinos for 63 days in 2003 and 65 days in 2005—usually on weekends and holidays, for 8 hours at a time
- playing video poker at casinos for more than 1,000 hours during the year, over 20 hours per week.

These examples show that you can forget about being a professional gambler unless you put in at least 35 hours per week gambling most weeks of the year. Moreover, as a rule, professional gamblers have no job other than gambling. If you have another job, it's likely the IRS will claim you're not a gambling professional.

### Profit motivation test

The fact that a person gambles full-time doesn't necessarily mean that he or she is a professional gambler. Lots of retired people gamble full-time, but would never consider themselves professionals; they gamble for entertainment. To qualify as a professional gambler, you must gamble *primarily to earn a profit*. You don't have to show a profit every year to qualify as a professional, but your primary purpose must be to make money, not to have fun gambling.

The IRS can't read your mind to see if you gamble to earn a profit or to have fun, and it certainly isn't going to take your word for it. The IRS looks at the following "objective" factors to determine whether you are behaving like a person who wants to earn a profit (and therefore, should be classified as a business). These factors can be found at Section 1.183-2(a) of the IRS income tax regulations.

You don't have to satisfy all of these factors to pass the test, but the more you satisfy the better off you'll be.

- **Whether you act like a business.** Among other things, acting like a business means you keep good books and other records and carry on your gambling activity in a professional manner.

- **Your expertise.** People who are in business to make money usually have some knowledge and skill relevant to the business. If they don't have it, they take steps to acquire it. Additionally, the more expertise an activity requires, the more likely it will be viewed as a business. For this reason, the IRS is more likely to view a poker player as a professional than someone who just plays slot machines. Indeed, the IRS has argued, albeit unsuccessfully, that anyone who only plays slots cannot expect to ever earn a profit.

- **The time and effort you spend.** Businesspeople work regularly and continuously at their businesses. As discussed above, you'll have trouble qualifying as a professional gambler unless you work at it full-time.

- **Your track record.** Having a track record of success in other businesses—whether or not they are related to your current gambling business—helps show that you are trying to make money in your current gambling venture.

- **Your history of profit and losses.** If you earn a profit from gambling in any three of five consecutive years, the IRS must presume that you are in business. This "statutory presumption" will help you if you're audited—but it doesn't guarantee the IRS won't give you trouble. Even if you meet the three-of-five test, the IRS can still claim that your gambling activity is not a business. This is particularly likely where the amount of your profits during your profitable years are small compared to your losses in the other losing years.

  You don't absolutely have to pass the three-of-five test to

be a professional gambler; but, if you never have profitable years, you'll have a hard time convincing the IRS you are in business.

- **Amount of occasional profits.** Even if you can't satisfy the three-of-five year profit test described above, earning a profit in at least some years helps show that you're in business. Earning a substantial profit, even after years of losses, can help show that you are trying to make a go of it. On the other hand, earning only small or occasional yearly profits when you have years of large losses tends to show that you aren't in it for the money.

- **Your personal wealth.** The IRS figures that you probably have a profit motive¾and are running a real business¾if you don't have a substantial income from sources other than gambling. After all, you'll need to earn money from your gambling venture to survive. On the other hand, the IRS may be suspicious if you have substantial income from other. Gambling doesn't have to be your only source of income, but it should be your main source.

- **Elements of personal recreation or entertainment.** The more fun you have at an activity, the less likely will the IRS view it as a business. This can make it harder for gamblers to establish that they are in business. This makes it particularly important to satisfy as many of the other factors as possible.

## Six ways to do to show you're in business

Here are six things you should do if you want the IRS to recognize you as a professional gambler.

**Keep good business records.** Keeping good records of your gambling winnings, losses, and expenses—and the time you spend gambling—is the single most important thing you can do to show that you want to earn a profit. Lack of records shows that you don't really care whether you make money or not, and is almost always fatal in an IRS audit.

**Keep a separate checking account.** Open a separate checking account for your gambling business. This will help you keep your personal and business expenses separate—another factor that shows you want to make money.

**Business address and cards.** Have a business office address or post office box. Get business cards and letterhead. It may seem like a minor matter, but obtaining business stationery and business cards shows that you think you are in business. Hobbyists ordinarily don't have such things.

**Create a business plan.** Draw up a business plan with a realistic profit and loss forecast—a projection of how much money your gambling business will bring in, your expenses, and how much profit you expect to make. The forecast should cover the next five or ten years. It should show you earning a profit some time in the future (although it doesn't have to be within five years). Both the IRS and courts are usually impressed by good business plans.

**Get expertise**. If you're already an expert gambler, you're a step ahead of the game. But if you aren't, you should take steps to thoroughly educate yourself by reading gambling books, practicing gambling online, and talking to gambling experts.

**Change strategies**. If you keep losing money, you should take steps to try to do better. This is what businesspeople do. For example, try switching to games with better odds, gamble at casinos with more cashback, or try betting on "overlays" (bets whose chances of success are underestimated by the typical casual gambler).

# Professional or Casual Gambler: Which Is Better?

If you qualify as a professional gambler, you inhabit an entirely different tax universe from casual gamblers. Some of these differences are good, some not so good. Whether being a professional is better taxwise than being a casual gambler depends on your personal circumstances.

First, the good: Unlike casual gamblers, professionals only report on their tax return their net income from gambling-that is, they get to subtract their losses (and other expenses) from their winnings. If a professional gambler's expenses are equal to or greater than his winnings, he'll have zero gambling income to list on his tax return and pay tax on.

Unlike casual gamblers, a professional's total winnings are not directly added to his adjusted gross income (AGI) without any deductions. Thus, a professional gambler will always have a lower AGI than a casual gambler who wins the same amount. Keeping your AGI low can help save many important tax deductions that casual gamblers can lose when their AGI is inflated by their total gambling winnings. (See Chapter 6).

In addition, professional gamblers get to deduct their business expenses from their winnings. These include not only their gambling losses, but expenses such as travel, hotels, dealer tips, and internet and cell phone costs. Professional gamblers can also deduct their health insurance costs and establish tax advantaged retirement accounts. Casual gamblers get no such deductions.

However, the professional's tax lot is not all good. Professional gamblers must pay the same taxes all small business owners must pay—this includes both income taxes and self-employment taxes. Self-employment taxes consist of a 12.4% Social Security tax up to an annual ceiling amount ($106,800 in 2010-2011), and a 2.9% Medicare tax on all net business income. That's a combined 15.3% tax on their income up to the annual ceiling. You must pay self-employment taxes if your net yearly earnings from self-employment are $400 or more. When you file your annual tax return, you must include IRS Form SE, showing how much self-employment tax you have to pay.

Casual gamblers don't have to pay self-employment taxes on their gambling winnings. For this reason, filing as a professional can result in more tax than filing as a casual gambler. On the plus side, a professional who pays enough into Social Security will be entitled to benefits when he or she reaches retirement age.

In addition, unlike all other businesses, professional gamblers are not allowed to deduct their losses against non-gambling income. For example, if you win $50,000 and have $60,000 in expenses (including your losses), you only get to deduct $50,000 of those expenses. You can't deduct the remaining $10,000 in expenses from other non-gambling income you may have, such as investment income or your spouse's income. Nor can you use the extra losses to deduct against your gambling income in future years. In effect, you get no tax benefit at all from the amount of gambling expenses that exceed your annual gambling income. (IRC Sec. 165(d).)

## Tax Deductions for Professional Gamblers

Professional gamblers pay the same taxes as other small business people, and they get the same tax deductions. When you're a gambling professional, you can deduct from your gambling income any expense that is reasonable, ordinary and necessary, and directly related to your gambling business. These include, but are not limited to:

- your gambling losses
- travel to and from casinos and other gambling establishments
- hotel and meal expenses while gambling away from home (meals are only 50% deductible)

- expenses for driving to casinos and other gambling establishments
- poker tournament entry fees
- time (seat rental) fees
- passport fee (for foreign trips)
- office supplies
- professional journals
- safe deposit box rental fees
- tips
- interest on loans for your gambling business
- home office expenses (subject to special limitations)
- accounting and legal fees (including the cost of this book)
- business equipment, such as computers, cell phones, or a car you use to travel to casinos (only partly deductible if you only use it part-time for business)
- the cost of education and seminars you attend to sharpen your gambling skills
- gambling software
- Internet connection costs.

Because they get to deduct all their expenses from their winnings, professional gamblers who win more than they lose can still end up with little or no net gambling income subject to tax. This is not the case for casual gamblers, who only get to deduct their losses as an itemized deduction, and get no deductions for other expenses.

*EXAMPLE: Ira is a gambling professional; his sister, Irene, is a casual gambler. Last year they both won $50,000 gambling,* *lost $40,000, and had $10,000 in expenses. Ira's net gambling income is zero, and he owes no tax. Irene must pay income tax on $10,000 of her winnings because she can only deduct her losses, not her other expenses.*

You need to keep careful track of all these expenses, and keep receipts, credit card records, cancelled checks or other proof you paid for them.

For more details on all the tax deductions available to small businesspeople, including gambling professionals, refer to *Deduct It: Lower Your Small Business Taxes*, by Stephen Fishman. It's available from nolo.com.

## Paying Estimated Taxes

Federal income and self-employment taxes are pay-as-you-go taxes. You must pay these taxes as you earn or receive income during the year. Unlike employees, who usually have their income and Social Security and Medicare tax withheld from their pay by their employers, self-employed people—including professional gamblers—normally pay their income and Social Security and Medicare taxes directly to the IRS. These tax payments are called estimated taxes and are usually made four times every year on IRS Form 1040-ES—on April 15, June 15, September 15 and January 15. You have to figure out how much to pay; the IRS won't do it for you.

## Filling Out Your Tax Return as a Professional Gambler

When you are a professional gambler, you must file an annual income tax return with the IRS showing your gambling business income and deductions for the year and how much estimated tax you've paid. You file IRS Form 1040, and include with it IRS Schedule C, *Profit or Loss From Business*. On Schedule C you list all your gambling income and expenses. You then subtract your total expenses (including gambling losses) from your gambling income. If you have a net profit, you add the amount to any other income you report on your Form 1040. If you don't have a profit, you'll have no gambling income to add to your 1040 or pay tax on.

Here is a sample tax return for professional gambler Jimmy T. Greek. In 2010 he had $100,000 in gambling winnings and $50,000 in losses. He had other deductible professional gambling expenses of $15,500. As you can see from his Schedule C, after subtracting all of his expenses he had net gambling income of $34,000. He added this amount to his other income on his Form 1040. Because he was self-employed, he was allowed to deduct the cost of his health insurance on this form. He also had to file Form SE to show that he had to pay $3,879 in self-employment taxes. His total tax due for the year was $6,266. He had $6,000 of tax withheld from casinos and reported on IRS Form W-2G, so he owed $266.

Form **1040** Department of the Treasury—Internal Revenue Service
**U.S. Individual Income Tax Return** **2010** (99) IRS Use Only—Do not write or staple in this space.

| | |
|---|---|
| For the year Jan. 1–Dec. 31, 2010, or other tax year beginning , 2010, ending , 20 | OMB No. 1545-0074 |

**Name, Address, and SSN**
(PRINT CLEARLY)

Your first name and initial: Jimmy T. — Last name: Greek
Your social security number: 1 1 1 1 1 1 1 1 1

If a joint return, spouse's first name and initial — Last name
Spouse's social security number

Home address (number and street). If you have a P.O. box, see instructions. 7777 Sunset Strip — Apt. no.

City, town or post office, state, and ZIP code. If you have a foreign address, see instructions. Los Angeles, CA 90000

▲ Make sure the SSN(s) above and on line 6c are correct.

See separate instructions.

Checking a box below will not change your tax or refund.

**Presidential Election Campaign** ► Check here if you, or your spouse if filing jointly, want $3 to go to this fund . . . ► ☐ You ☐ Spouse

**Filing Status**
Check only one box.

1 ☐ Single
2 ☐ Married filing jointly (even if only one had income)
3 ☐ Married filing separately. Enter spouse's SSN above and full name here. ►
4 ☐ Head of household (with qualifying person). (See instructions.) If the qualifying person is a child but not your dependent, enter this child's name here. ►
5 ☐ Qualifying widow(er) with dependent child

**Exemptions**

6a ☐ Yourself. If someone can claim you as a dependent, do not check box 6a .
b ☐ Spouse
c Dependents:
(1) First name  Last name
(2) Dependent's social security number
(3) Dependent's relationship to you
(4) ✓ If child under age 17 qualifying for child tax credit (see page 15)

If more than four dependents, see instructions and check here ► ☐

Boxes checked on 6a and 6b
No. of children on 6c who:
• lived with you
• did not live with you due to divorce or separation (see instructions)
Dependents on 6c not entered above
Add numbers on lines above ► ☐

d Total number of exemptions claimed . . . . . . . . . . . . . . . .

**Income**

Attach Form(s) W-2 here. Also attach Forms W-2G and 1099-R if tax was withheld.

If you did not get a W-2, see page 20.

Enclose, but do not attach, any payment. Also, please use Form 1040-V.

|  |  |  |
|---|---|---|
| 7 | Wages, salaries, tips, etc. Attach Form(s) W-2 | 7 |
| 8a | Taxable interest. Attach Schedule B if required | 8a |
| b | Tax-exempt interest. Do not include on line 8a . 8b | |
| 9a | Ordinary dividends. Attach Schedule B if required | 9a |
| b | Qualified dividends . 9b | |
| 10 | Taxable refunds, credits, or offsets of state and local income taxes | 10 |
| 11 | Alimony received | 11 |
| 12 | Business income or (loss). Attach Schedule C or C-EZ | 12 | 34,000 |
| 13 | Capital gain or (loss). Attach Schedule D if required. If not required, check here ► ☐ | 13 |
| 14 | Other gains or (losses). Attach Form 4797 | 14 |
| 15a | IRA distributions . 15a | b Taxable amount | 15b |
| 16a | Pensions and annuities . 16a | b Taxable amount | 16b |
| 17 | Rental real estate, royalties, partnerships, S corporations, trusts, etc. Attach Schedule E | 17 |
| 18 | Farm income or (loss). Attach Schedule F | 18 |
| 19 | Unemployment compensation | 19 |
| 20a | Social security benefits . 20a | b Taxable amount | 20b |
| 21 | Other income. List type and amount | 21 |
| 22 | Combine the amounts in the far right column for lines 7 through 21. This is your total income ► | 22 | 34,000 |

**Adjusted Gross Income**

|  |  | |  |
|---|---|---|---|
| 23 | Educator expenses | 23 | |
| 24 | Certain business expenses of reservists, performing artists, and fee-basis government officials. Attach Form 2106 or 2106-EZ | 24 | |
| 25 | Health savings account deduction. Attach Form 8889 | 25 | |
| 26 | Moving expenses. Attach Form 3903 | 26 | |
| 27 | One-half of self-employment tax. Attach Schedule SE | 27 | 1,940 |
| 28 | Self-employed SEP, SIMPLE, and qualified plans | 28 | |
| 29 | Self-employed health insurance deduction | 29 | 4000 |
| 30 | Penalty on early withdrawal of savings | 30 | |
| 31a | Alimony paid b Recipient's SSN ► | 31a | |
| 32 | IRA deduction | 32 | |
| 33 | Student loan interest deduction | 33 | |
| 34 | Tuition and fees. Attach Form 8917 | 34 | |
| 35 | Domestic production activities deduction. Attach Form 8903 | 35 | |
| 36 | Add lines 23 through 31a and 32 through 35 | 36 | 5,940 |
| 37 | Subtract line 36 from line 22. This is your adjusted gross income ► | 37 | 28,060 |

For Disclosure, Privacy Act, and Paperwork Reduction Act Notice, see separate instructions. Cat. No. 11320B Form **1040** (2010)

Form 1040 (2010)

Page **2**

| Tax and Credits | 38 | Amount from line 37 (adjusted gross income) | | | 38 | |
|---|---|---|---|---|---|---|
| | 39a | Check { ☐ You were born before January 2, 1946, ☐ Blind. } Total boxes ☐ Spouse was born before January 2, 1946, ☐ Blind. } checked ► 39a ☐ | | | | |
| | b | If your spouse itemizes on a separate return or you were a dual-status alien, check here ► 39b ☐ | | | | |
| | 40 | Itemized deductions (from Schedule A) or your standard deduction (see instructions) | | | 40 | 5,700 |
| | 41 | Subtract line 40 from line 38 | | | 41 | 22,360 |
| | 42 | Exemptions. Multiply $3,650 by the number on line 6d | | | 42 | 3,650 |
| | 43 | Taxable income. Subtract line 42 from line 41. If line 42 is more than line 41, enter -0- | | | 43 | 18,710 |
| | 44 | Tax (see instructions). Check if any tax is from: a ☐ Form(s) 8814 b ☐ Form 4972 | | | 44 | 2,387 |
| | 45 | Alternative minimum tax (see instructions). Attach Form 6251 | | | 45 | |
| | 46 | Add lines 44 and 45 | | ► | 46 | |
| | 47 | Foreign tax credit. Attach Form 1116 if required | 47 | | | |
| | 48 | Credit for child and dependent care expenses. Attach Form 2441 | 48 | | | |
| | 49 | Education credits from Form 8863, line 23 | 49 | | | |
| | 50 | Retirement savings contributions credit. Attach Form 8880 | 50 | | | |
| | 51 | Child tax credit (see instructions) | 51 | | | |
| | 52 | Residential energy credits. Attach Form 5695 | 52 | | | |
| | 53 | Other credits from Form: a ☐ 3800 b ☐ 8801 c ☐ | 53 | | | |
| | 54 | Add lines 47 through 53. These are your total credits | | | 54 | |
| | 55 | Subtract line 54 from line 46. If line 54 is more than line 46, enter -0- | | ► | 55 | 2,387 |
| Other Taxes | 56 | Self-employment tax. Attach Schedule SE | | | 56 | 3,879 |
| | 57 | Unreported social security and Medicare tax from Form: a ☐ 4137 b ☐ 8919 | | | 57 | |
| | 58 | Additional tax on IRAs, other qualified retirement plans, etc. Attach Form 5329 if required | | | 58 | |
| | 59 | a ☐ Form(s) W-2, box 9 b ☐ Schedule H c ☐ Form 8405, line 16 | | | 59 | |
| | 60 | Add lines 55 through 59. This is your total tax | | ► | 60 | 6,266 |
| Payments | 61 | Federal income tax withheld from Forms W-2 and 1099 | 61 | 6000 | | |
| | 62 | 2010 estimated tax payments and amount applied from 2009 return | 62 | | | |
| | 63 | Making work pay credit. Attach Schedule M | 63 | | | |
| If you have a qualifying child, attach Schedule EIC. | 64a | Earned income credit (EIC) | 64a | | | |
| | b | Nontaxable combat pay election 64b | | | | |
| | 65 | Additional child tax credit. Attach Form 8812 | 65 | | | |
| | 66 | American opportunity credit from Form 8863, line 14 | 66 | | | |
| | 67 | First-time homebuyer credit from Form 5405, line 10 | 67 | | | |
| | 68 | Amount paid with request for extension to file | 68 | | | |
| | 69 | Excess social security and tier 1 RRTA tax withheld | 69 | | | |
| | 70 | Credit for federal tax on fuels. Attach Form 4136 | 70 | | | |
| | 71 | Credits from Form: a ☐ 2439 b ☐ 8839 c ☐ 8801 d ☐ 8885 | 71 | | | |
| | 72 | Add lines 61, 62, 63, 64a, and 65 through 71. These are your total payments | | ► | 72 | 6,000 |
| Refund | 73 | If line 72 is more than line 60, subtract line 60 from line 72. This is the amount you overpaid | | | 73 | |
| | 74a | Amount of line 73 you want refunded to you. If Form 8888 is attached, check here ► ☐ | | | 74a | |
| Direct deposit? See instructions. | b | Routing number ► c Type: ☐ Checking ☐ Savings | | | | |
| | d | Account number | | | | |
| | 75 | Amount of line 73 you want applied to your 2011 estimated tax ► | 75 | | | |
| Amount You Owe | 76 | Amount you owe. Subtract line 72 from line 60. For details on how to pay, see instructions ► | | | 76 | 266 |
| | 77 | Estimated tax penalty (see instructions) | 77 | | | |

| Third Party Designee | Do you want to allow another person to discuss this return with the IRS (see instructions)? ☐ Yes. Complete below. ☐ No |
|---|---|
| | Designee's name ► Phone no. ► Personal identification number (PIN) ► |

| Sign Here | Under penalties of perjury, I declare that I have examined this return and accompanying schedules and statements, and to the best of my knowledge and belief, they are true, correct, and complete. Declaration of preparer (other than taxpayer) is based on all information of which preparer has any knowledge. |
|---|---|
| Joint return? See page 12. Keep a copy for your records. | Your signature — Date — Your occupation **Professional Gambler** — Daytime phone number |
| | Spouse's signature. If a joint return, both must sign. — Date — Spouse's occupation |

| Paid Preparer Use Only | Print/Type preparer's name — Preparer's signature — Date — Check ☐ if self-employed — PTIN |
|---|---|
| | Firm's name ► — Firm's EIN ► |
| | Firm's address ► — Phone no. |

Form **1040** (2010)

**SCHEDULE C**
**(Form 1040)**

Department of the Treasury
Internal Revenue Service (99)

**Profit or Loss From Business**
(Sole Proprietorship)
► Partnerships, joint ventures, etc., generally must file Form 1065 or 1065-B.
► Attach to Form 1040, 1040NR, or 1041. ► See Instructions for Schedule C (Form 1040).

OMB No. 1545-0074

**2010**

Attachment
Sequence No. **09**

Name of proprietor
Jimmy T. Greek

Social security number (SSN)
222-22-2222

A Principal business or profession, including product or service (see instructions)
Professional Gambler

B Enter code from pages C-9, 10, & 11
►

C Business name. If no separate business name, leave blank.

D Employer ID number (EIN), if any

E Business address (including suite or room no.) ► 7777 Sunset Strip
City, town or post office, state, and ZIP code    Los Angeles, CA 90000

F Accounting method: (1) ☑ Cash (2) ☐ Accrual (3) ☐ Other (specify) ►

G Did you "materially participate" in the operation of this business during 2010? If "No," see instructions for limit on losses    ☑ Yes    ☐ No

H If you started or acquired this business during 2010, check here    ► ☐

**Part I   Income**

| | | | |
|---|---|---|---|
| 1 | Gross receipts or sales. Caution. See instructions and check the box if: • This income was reported to you on Form W-2 and the "Statutory employee" box on that form was checked, or • You are a member of a qualified joint venture reporting only rental real estate income not subject to self-employment tax. Also see instructions for limit on losses ► ☐ | 1 | 100,000 |
| 2 | Returns and allowances | 2 | |
| 3 | Subtract line 2 from line 1 | 3 | 100,000 |
| 4 | Cost of goods sold (from line 42 on page 2) | 4 | |
| 5 | Gross profit. Subtract line 4 from line 3 | 5 | 100,000 |
| 6 | Other income, including federal and state gasoline or fuel tax credit or refund (see instructions) | 6 | |
| 7 | Gross income. Add lines 5 and 6 ► | 7 | 100,000 |

**Part II   Expenses.** Enter expenses for business use of your home **only** on line 30.

| | | | | | | |
|---|---|---|---|---|---|---|
| 8 | Advertising | 8 | | 18 | Office expense | 18 | |
| 9 | Car and truck expenses (see instructions) | 9 | | 19 | Pension and profit-sharing plans | 19 | |
| 10 | Commissions and fees | 10 | | 20 | Rent or lease (see instructions): | | |
| 11 | Contract labor (see instructions) | 11 | | a | Vehicles, machinery, and equipment | 20a | |
| 12 | Depletion | 12 | | b | Other business property | 20b | |
| 13 | Depreciation and section 179 expense deduction (not included in Part III) (see instructions) | 13 | | 21 | Repairs and maintenance | 21 | |
| | | | | 22 | Supplies (not included in Part III) | 22 | 250 |
| | | | | 23 | Taxes and licenses | 23 | |
| | | | | 24 | Travel, meals, and entertainment: | | |
| 14 | Employee benefit programs (other than on line 19) | 14 | | a | Travel | 24a | 10,000 |
| 15 | Insurance (other than health) | 15 | | b | Deductible meals and entertainment (see instructions) | 24b | 5,000 |
| 16 | Interest: | | | 25 | Utilities | 25 | |
| a | Mortgage (paid to banks, etc.) | 16a | | 26 | Wages (less employment credits) | 26 | |
| b | Other | 16b | | 27 | Other expenses (from line 48 on page 2) | 27 | 50,500 |
| 17 | Legal and professional services | 17 | 250 | | | | |

| | | | |
|---|---|---|---|
| 28 | Total expenses before expenses for business use of home. Add lines 8 through 27 ► | 28 | 66,000 |
| 29 | Tentative profit or (loss). Subtract line 28 from line 7 | 29 | 34,000 |
| 30 | Expenses for business use of your home. Attach Form 8829 | 30 | |
| 31 | Net profit or (loss). Subtract line 30 from line 29. • If a profit, enter on both Form 1040, line 12, and Schedule SE, line 2, or on Form 1040NR, line 13 (if you checked the box on line 1, see instructions). Estates and trusts, enter on Form 1041, line 3. • If a loss, you must go to line 32. | 31 | 34,000 |
| 32 | If you have a loss, check the box that describes your investment in this activity (see instructions). • If you checked 32a, enter the loss on both Form 1040, line 12, and Schedule SE, line 2, or on Form 1040NR, line 13 (if you checked the box on line 1, see the line 31 instructions). Estates and trusts, enter on Form 1041, line 3. • If you checked 32b, you must attach Form 6198. Your loss may be limited. | 32a ☐ All investment is at risk. 32b ☐ Some investment is not at risk. | |

For Paperwork Reduction Act Notice, see your tax return instructions.    Cat. No. 11334P    Schedule C (Form 1040) 2010

Schedule C (Form 1040) 2010 Page **2**

**Part III**   Cost of Goods Sold (see instructions)

33   Method(s) used to
value closing inventory.    a ☐ Cost     b ☐ Lower of cost or market     c ☐ Other (attach explanation)

34   Was there any change in determining quantities, costs, or valuations between opening and closing inventory?
If "Yes," attach explanation . . . . . . . . . . . . . . . . . . . . . . . . . . . . . . . ☐ Yes    ☐ No

| | | |
|---|---|---|
| 35   Inventory at beginning of year. If different from last year's closing inventory, attach explanation | 35 | |
| 36   Purchases less cost of items withdrawn for personal use | 36 | |
| 37   Cost of labor. Do not include any amounts paid to yourself | 37 | |
| 38   Materials and supplies | 38 | |
| 39   Other costs | 39 | |
| 40   Add lines 35 through 39 | 40 | |
| 41   Inventory at end of year | 41 | |
| 42   **Cost of goods sold.** Subtract line 41 from line 40. Enter the result here and on page 1, line 4 | 42 | |

**Part IV**   Information on Your Vehicle. Complete this part **only** if you are claiming car or truck expenses on line 9 and are not required to file Form 4562 for this business. See the instructions for line 13 to find out if you must file Form 4562.

43   When did you place your vehicle in service for business purposes? (month, day, year) ▶   /   /

44   Of the total number of miles you drove your vehicle during 2010, enter the number of miles you used your vehicle for:

a   Business _____   b   Commuting (see instructions) _____   c   Other _____

45   Was your vehicle available for personal use during off-duty hours? . . . . . . . . . . . . . ☐ Yes    ☐ No

46   Do you (or your spouse) have another vehicle available for personal use? . . . . . . . . . . . ☐ Yes    ☐ No

47a   Do you have evidence to support your deduction? . . . . . . . . . . . . . . . . . . . . ☐ Yes    ☐ No

b   If "Yes," is the evidence written? . . . . . . . . . . . . . . . . . . . . . . . . . ☐ Yes    ☐ No

**Part V**   Other Expenses. List below business expenses not included on lines 8–26 or line 30.

| | |
|---|---|
| Gambling losses | 50,000 |
| Poker education materials | 500 |
| | |
| | |
| | |
| | |
| | |
| | |
| | |

| | | |
|---|---|---|
| 48   Total other expenses. Enter here and on page 1, line 27 | 48 | 50,500 |

Schedule C (Form 1040) 2010

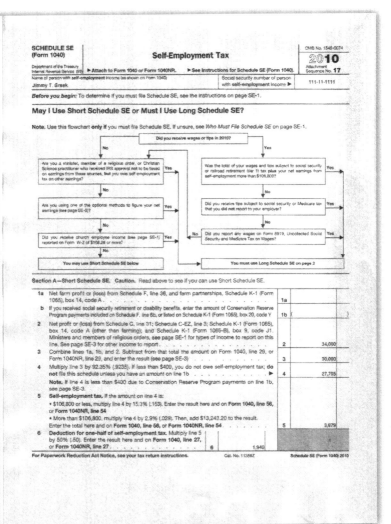

SCHEDULE SE
(Form 1040)

Department of the Treasury
Internal Revenue Service (99)

**Self-Employment Tax**

► Attach to Form 1040 or Form 1040NR.    ► See Instructions for Schedule SE (Form 1040).

OMB No. 1545-0074

2010

Attachment
Sequence No. **17**

Name of person with self-employment income (as shown on Form 1040)
Jimmy T. Greek

Social security number of person
with self-employment income ►    111-11-1111

*Before you begin:* To determine if you must file Schedule SE, see the instructions on page SE-1.

## May I Use Short Schedule SE or Must I Use Long Schedule SE?

**Note.** Use this flowchart *only* if you must file Schedule SE. If unsure, see *Who Must File Schedule SE* on page SE-1.

**Section A—Short Schedule SE. Caution.** Read above to see if you can use Short Schedule SE.

| | | | |
|---|---|---|---|
| 1a | Net farm profit or (loss) from Schedule F, line 36, and farm partnerships, Schedule K-1 (Form 1065), box 14, code A . . . . . . . . . . . . . . . . | 1a | |
| b | If you received social security retirement or disability benefits, enter the amount of Conservation Reserve Program payments included on Schedule F, line 6b, or listed on Schedule K-1 (Form 1065), box 20, code Y | 1b ( | ) |
| 2 | Net profit or (loss) from Schedule C, line 31; Schedule C-EZ, line 3; Schedule K-1 (Form 1065), box 14, code A (other than farming); and Schedule K-1 (Form 1065-B), box 9, code J1. Ministers and members of religious orders, see page SE-1 for types of income to report on this line. See page SE-3 for other income to report . . . . . . . . . . . . . . . . | 2 | 34,000 |
| 3 | Combine lines 1a, 1b, and 2. Subtract from that total the amount on Form 1040, line 29, or Form 1040NR, line 29, and enter the result (see page SE-3) . . . . . . . . . . | 3 | 30,000 |
| 4 | Multiply line 3 by 92.35% (.9235). If less than $400, you do not owe self-employment tax; do **not** file this schedule unless you have an amount on line 1b . . . . . . . . . . ► | 4 | 27,705 |
| | **Note.** If line 4 is less than $400 due to Conservation Reserve Program payments on line 1b, see page SE-3. | | |
| 5 | Self-employment tax. If the amount on line 4 is:<br>• $106,800 or less, multiply line 4 by 15.3% (.153). Enter the result here and on **Form 1040, line 56,** or **Form 1040NR, line 54**<br>• More than $106,800, multiply line 4 by 2.9% (.029). Then, add $13,243.20 to the result. Enter the total here and on **Form 1040, line 56, or Form 1040NR, line 54** . . . . . . | 5 | 3,879 |
| 6 | Deduction for one-half of self-employment tax. Multiply line 5 by 50% (.50). Enter the result here and on **Form 1040, line 27,** or **Form 1040NR, line 27** . . . . . . . . . . | 6 | 1,940 |

For Paperwork Reduction Act Notice, see your tax return instructions.    Cat. No. 11358Z    Schedule SE (Form 1040) 2010

# Appendix: Gambling Log

| Date | Time | Location | Game | Net Win | Net Loss | W-2Gs | Accompanied by |
|------|------|----------|------|---------|----------|-------|----------------|
|      |      |          |      |         |          |       |                |
|      |      |          |      |         |          |       |                |
|      |      |          |      |         |          |       |                |
|      |      |          |      |         |          |       |                |
|      |      |          |      |         |          |       |                |
|      |      |          |      |         |          |       |                |
|      |      |          |      |         |          |       |                |
|      |      |          |      |         |          |       |                |
|      |      |          |      |         |          |       |                |
|      |      |          |      |         |          |       |                |
|      |      |          |      |         |          |       |                |
|      |      |          |      |         |          |       |                |
|      |      |          |      |         |          |       |                |
|      |      |          |      |         |          |       |                |
|      |      |          |      |         |          |       |                |
|      |      |          |      |         |          |       |                |
|      |      |          |      |         |          |       |                |
|      |      |          |      |         |          |       |                |
|      |      |          |      |         |          |       |                |
|      |      |          |      |         |          |       |                |
|      |      |          |      |         |          |       |                |
|      |      |          |      |         |          |       |                |
|      |      |          |      |         |          |       |                |
|      |      |          |      |         |          |       |                |

| Date | Time | Location | Game | Net Win | Net Loss | W-2Gs | Accompanied by |
|------|------|----------|------|---------|----------|-------|----------------|
|      |      |          |      |         |          |       |                |
|      |      |          |      |         |          |       |                |
|      |      |          |      |         |          |       |                |
|      |      |          |      |         |          |       |                |
|      |      |          |      |         |          |       |                |
|      |      |          |      |         |          |       |                |
|      |      |          |      |         |          |       |                |
|      |      |          |      |         |          |       |                |
|      |      |          |      |         |          |       |                |
|      |      |          |      |         |          |       |                |
|      |      |          |      |         |          |       |                |
|      |      |          |      |         |          |       |                |
|      |      |          |      |         |          |       |                |
|      |      |          |      |         |          |       |                |
|      |      |          |      |         |          |       |                |
|      |      |          |      |         |          |       |                |
|      |      |          |      |         |          |       |                |
|      |      |          |      |         |          |       |                |
|      |      |          |      |         |          |       |                |
|      |      |          |      |         |          |       |                |
|      |      |          |      |         |          |       |                |
|      |      |          |      |         |          |       |                |

| Date | Time | Location | Game | Net Win | Net Loss | W-2Gs | Accompanied by |
|------|------|----------|------|---------|----------|-------|----------------|
|      |      |          |      |         |          |       |                |
|      |      |          |      |         |          |       |                |
|      |      |          |      |         |          |       |                |
|      |      |          |      |         |          |       |                |
|      |      |          |      |         |          |       |                |
|      |      |          |      |         |          |       |                |
|      |      |          |      |         |          |       |                |
|      |      |          |      |         |          |       |                |
|      |      |          |      |         |          |       |                |
|      |      |          |      |         |          |       |                |
|      |      |          |      |         |          |       |                |
|      |      |          |      |         |          |       |                |
|      |      |          |      |         |          |       |                |
|      |      |          |      |         |          |       |                |
|      |      |          |      |         |          |       |                |
|      |      |          |      |         |          |       |                |
|      |      |          |      |         |          |       |                |
|      |      |          |      |         |          |       |                |
|      |      |          |      |         |          |       |                |
|      |      |          |      |         |          |       |                |

| Date | Time | Location | Game | Net Win | Net Loss | W-2Gs | Accompanied by |
|------|------|----------|------|---------|----------|-------|----------------|
|      |      |          |      |         |          |       |                |
|      |      |          |      |         |          |       |                |
|      |      |          |      |         |          |       |                |
|      |      |          |      |         |          |       |                |
|      |      |          |      |         |          |       |                |
|      |      |          |      |         |          |       |                |
|      |      |          |      |         |          |       |                |
|      |      |          |      |         |          |       |                |
|      |      |          |      |         |          |       |                |
|      |      |          |      |         |          |       |                |
|      |      |          |      |         |          |       |                |
|      |      |          |      |         |          |       |                |
|      |      |          |      |         |          |       |                |
|      |      |          |      |         |          |       |                |
|      |      |          |      |         |          |       |                |
|      |      |          |      |         |          |       |                |
|      |      |          |      |         |          |       |                |
|      |      |          |      |         |          |       |                |
|      |      |          |      |         |          |       |                |
|      |      |          |      |         |          |       |                |
|      |      |          |      |         |          |       |                |
|      |      |          |      |         |          |       |                |
|      |      |          |      |         |          |       |                |
|      |      |          |      |         |          |       |                |

| Date | Time | Location | Game | Net Win | Net Loss | W-2Gs | Accompanied by |
|------|------|----------|------|---------|----------|-------|----------------|
|      |      |          |      |         |          |       |                |
|      |      |          |      |         |          |       |                |
|      |      |          |      |         |          |       |                |
|      |      |          |      |         |          |       |                |
|      |      |          |      |         |          |       |                |
|      |      |          |      |         |          |       |                |
|      |      |          |      |         |          |       |                |
|      |      |          |      |         |          |       |                |
|      |      |          |      |         |          |       |                |
|      |      |          |      |         |          |       |                |
|      |      |          |      |         |          |       |                |
|      |      |          |      |         |          |       |                |
|      |      |          |      |         |          |       |                |
|      |      |          |      |         |          |       |                |
|      |      |          |      |         |          |       |                |
|      |      |          |      |         |          |       |                |
|      |      |          |      |         |          |       |                |
|      |      |          |      |         |          |       |                |
|      |      |          |      |         |          |       |                |
|      |      |          |      |         |          |       |                |
|      |      |          |      |         |          |       |                |
|      |      |          |      |         |          |       |                |
|      |      |          |      |         |          |       |                |
|      |      |          |      |         |          |       |                |
|      |      |          |      |         |          |       |                |
|      |      |          |      |         |          |       |                |

| Date | Time | Location | Game | Net Win | Net Loss | W-2Gs | Accompanied by |
|------|------|----------|------|---------|----------|-------|----------------|
|      |      |          |      |         |          |       |                |
|      |      |          |      |         |          |       |                |
|      |      |          |      |         |          |       |                |
|      |      |          |      |         |          |       |                |
|      |      |          |      |         |          |       |                |
|      |      |          |      |         |          |       |                |
|      |      |          |      |         |          |       |                |
|      |      |          |      |         |          |       |                |
|      |      |          |      |         |          |       |                |
|      |      |          |      |         |          |       |                |
|      |      |          |      |         |          |       |                |
|      |      |          |      |         |          |       |                |
|      |      |          |      |         |          |       |                |
|      |      |          |      |         |          |       |                |
|      |      |          |      |         |          |       |                |
|      |      |          |      |         |          |       |                |
|      |      |          |      |         |          |       |                |
|      |      |          |      |         |          |       |                |
|      |      |          |      |         |          |       |                |
|      |      |          |      |         |          |       |                |
|      |      |          |      |         |          |       |                |
|      |      |          |      |         |          |       |                |
|      |      |          |      |         |          |       |                |
|      |      |          |      |         |          |       |                |

| Date | Time | Location | Game | Net Win | Net Loss | W-2Gs | Accompanied by |
|------|------|----------|------|---------|----------|-------|----------------|
|      |      |          |      |         |          |       |                |
|      |      |          |      |         |          |       |                |
|      |      |          |      |         |          |       |                |
|      |      |          |      |         |          |       |                |
|      |      |          |      |         |          |       |                |
|      |      |          |      |         |          |       |                |
|      |      |          |      |         |          |       |                |
|      |      |          |      |         |          |       |                |
|      |      |          |      |         |          |       |                |
|      |      |          |      |         |          |       |                |
|      |      |          |      |         |          |       |                |
|      |      |          |      |         |          |       |                |
|      |      |          |      |         |          |       |                |
|      |      |          |      |         |          |       |                |
|      |      |          |      |         |          |       |                |
|      |      |          |      |         |          |       |                |
|      |      |          |      |         |          |       |                |
|      |      |          |      |         |          |       |                |
|      |      |          |      |         |          |       |                |
|      |      |          |      |         |          |       |                |
|      |      |          |      |         |          |       |                |
|      |      |          |      |         |          |       |                |
|      |      |          |      |         |          |       |                |
|      |      |          |      |         |          |       |                |

| Date | Time | Location | Game | Net Win | Net Loss | W-2Gs | Accompanied by |
|------|------|----------|------|---------|----------|-------|----------------|
|      |      |          |      |         |          |       |                |
|      |      |          |      |         |          |       |                |
|      |      |          |      |         |          |       |                |
|      |      |          |      |         |          |       |                |
|      |      |          |      |         |          |       |                |
|      |      |          |      |         |          |       |                |
|      |      |          |      |         |          |       |                |
|      |      |          |      |         |          |       |                |
|      |      |          |      |         |          |       |                |
|      |      |          |      |         |          |       |                |
|      |      |          |      |         |          |       |                |
|      |      |          |      |         |          |       |                |
|      |      |          |      |         |          |       |                |
|      |      |          |      |         |          |       |                |
|      |      |          |      |         |          |       |                |
|      |      |          |      |         |          |       |                |
|      |      |          |      |         |          |       |                |
|      |      |          |      |         |          |       |                |
|      |      |          |      |         |          |       |                |
|      |      |          |      |         |          |       |                |
|      |      |          |      |         |          |       |                |
|      |      |          |      |         |          |       |                |
|      |      |          |      |         |          |       |                |

| Date | Time | Location | Game | Net Win | Net Loss | W-2Gs | Accompanied by |
|------|------|----------|------|---------|----------|-------|----------------|
|      |      |          |      |         |          |       |                |
|      |      |          |      |         |          |       |                |
|      |      |          |      |         |          |       |                |
|      |      |          |      |         |          |       |                |
|      |      |          |      |         |          |       |                |
|      |      |          |      |         |          |       |                |
|      |      |          |      |         |          |       |                |
|      |      |          |      |         |          |       |                |
|      |      |          |      |         |          |       |                |
|      |      |          |      |         |          |       |                |
|      |      |          |      |         |          |       |                |
|      |      |          |      |         |          |       |                |
|      |      |          |      |         |          |       |                |
|      |      |          |      |         |          |       |                |
|      |      |          |      |         |          |       |                |
|      |      |          |      |         |          |       |                |
|      |      |          |      |         |          |       |                |
|      |      |          |      |         |          |       |                |
|      |      |          |      |         |          |       |                |
|      |      |          |      |         |          |       |                |
|      |      |          |      |         |          |       |                |
|      |      |          |      |         |          |       |                |

| Date | Time | Location | Game | Net Win | Net Loss | W-2Gs | Accompanied by |
|------|------|----------|------|---------|----------|-------|----------------|
|  |  |  |  |  |  |  |  |
|  |  |  |  |  |  |  |  |
|  |  |  |  |  |  |  |  |
|  |  |  |  |  |  |  |  |
|  |  |  |  |  |  |  |  |
|  |  |  |  |  |  |  |  |
|  |  |  |  |  |  |  |  |
|  |  |  |  |  |  |  |  |
|  |  |  |  |  |  |  |  |
|  |  |  |  |  |  |  |  |
|  |  |  |  |  |  |  |  |
|  |  |  |  |  |  |  |  |
|  |  |  |  |  |  |  |  |
|  |  |  |  |  |  |  |  |
|  |  |  |  |  |  |  |  |
|  |  |  |  |  |  |  |  |
|  |  |  |  |  |  |  |  |
|  |  |  |  |  |  |  |  |
|  |  |  |  |  |  |  |  |
|  |  |  |  |  |  |  |  |

# Index

Made in the USA
Lexington, KY
29 August 2013